AMBUSHED

AT SUNSET

AMBUSHED
AT SUNSET

Coping With Mature
Adult Temptations

Dr. John Gilmore

LANGMARC PUBLISHING • San Antonio, Texas

AMBUSHED AT SUNSET

COPING WITH MATURE ADULT TEMPTATIONS
DR. JOHN GILMORE

Editor: James D. Qualben, Ph.D.
Cover: Michael Qualben

Several Scripture translations warrant acknowledgment with appreciation.

Scripture quotations from *The Holy Bible, New International Version* R NIV R. © 1973, 1978, 1984 by International Bible Society. Used by permission of Zondervan Publishing House. All rights reserved.

Scripture quotations from *New American Standard Bible* R © The Lockman Foundation 1960, 1962, 1963, 1971, 1973, 1975, 1977. Used by permission.

Scripture quotations from *Revised Standard Version of the Bible* © 1946, 1952, and 1971 by Division of Christian Education of the National Council of the Churches of Christ in the USA. Used by permission.

Scripture quotations from *New Revised Standard Version of the Bible* © 1989 by the Division of Christian Education of the National Council of Churches of Christ in the USA. All rights reserved: Used by permission

Other translations used: New King James (NKJV), Thomas Nelson, Nashville, TN © 1982; *Good News Bible* (GNB), American Bible Society, New York, NY © 1966, 1971, 1976; James Moffett translations of *The Holy Bible,* Harper & Row Publishers, Inc. © 1922, 1924, 1925, 1926, 1955.

Published by
LangMarc Publishing
P.O. Box 33817
San Antonio, Texas 78265

Library of Congress Cataloging-in-Publication Data
Gilmore, John, 1934-
        Ambushed at sunset : coping with mature adult
temptations / by John Gilmore.
                p. cm.
        Includes bibliographical references.
        ISBN 1-880292-59-9
        1. Aged--Religious life. 2. Temptation. I. Title.
        BV4580.G55   1998   97-52198
        248.8'5--dc21   CIP

DEDICATION

TO

❧ ROBERTA ❧

my lovely and loving
Fifty-something Wife
Companion
Friend

Mother of our three children
Contributor to sharp thinking
Clear writing
My ballast in rough waters
My chief inspiration
and
Fellow pilgrim in living
for the
Glory of God

CONTENTS

PREFACE

Over fifty? If not, it may be on your horizon. Or you may have passed it. When you hit the BIG 5 0, you probably get funny cards, maybe a cake with fifty flaming candles, perhaps even a sign on your lawn—erected by a gleeful spouse—that says "Happy Half Century."

At fifty retirement options emerge. Early retirement is attractive. Haven't we all been tempted to quit early and enjoy the rest of life without the burdens of a nine-to-five routine?

Is early retirement really a temptation? How can potential good be a true temptation if temptation is solicitation to do evil? Some discover after a while that leaving full-time employment was premature. Was their early-out the best choice they ever made? Do difficult consequences mean it was a bad choice? What makes the difference? Such issues lead us to the heart of what constitutes temptation.

The pluses of early retirement lure us. (We can be more lured *in* our leisure years than lured *into* them.) All too often, the really difficult temptations are those *within* retirement!

Grant that a non-judgmental environment best suits evil's growth. Grant that in the retired state an ideal freedom from regimentation exists. But alas, such atmospheres can become a feeding ground for the bacteria of evil's rapid growth.

Wait a minute, we think, "I know a saintly senior." A case can be made that many seniors demonstrate a detachment from and victory over sin. Godly seniors are not rare. Sherwood Wirt noted, "As people grow older their tempers calm down. They are not upset as they once were, nor do they react the way they did when they were younger."[1]

Is it right to assume, however, that those past fifty start rising above temptations? A fact of life is that the best of Christians throughout the centuries testify to an ongoing battle with inner evil—regardless of their age. Even octogenarian Christian Sherwood Wirt confessed to having been tricked by Satan.[2]

We all want to end life as moral winners. But that can't happen unless we advance in spiritual knowledge. What better golden opportunities for knowing and growing in Christ than in retirement? Make your last years your spiritually best years.

Ambushed at Sunset focuses on conquering temptations that hinder growth and devotion in older adults. These studies developed over many years. Input from others was important in fine tuning. My thanks goes to Madisonville Baptist Church, Ohio, where these topics were first explored. Also, my appreciation goes to those who took part in two seminars I conducted at Cincinnati's Christian Leaders and Sunday School Convention (C.L.A.S.S.) and to the Wyoming Baptist Church where I conducted a six-week seminar on senior temptations.

Senior ministries in a variety of traditional Protestant churches are looking for entry-level interaction on moral issues among seniors. May what follows encourage intentional and inspirational programming for seniors in your church.

Dr. John Gilmore
Kerux Kabin Ministries[3]
May 16, 1997

1

MYTHS AND REALITY
OF TEMPTATIONS

...[I can't] think of any [hardships of growing old], except that I can no longer ride horseback all day and I can no longer dance all night. Other than that the limitations of age came upon me so gradually that I was hardly aware of them until people began to tell me there were certain things I should no longer try to do. I don't care. Maybe I would have to slow down, but I refused to cut down. I have too many interests. I have my work. I have my family. I have my friends. I have the many "causes" that are important to me and make each day vital. I have lived a long time. I have learned a great deal, and I feel I have something to say to people. And I always welcome the chance to speak my piece....I'm having too much fun to let old age make me submit to a rocking chair and a shawl. I still have a lot of living to do.[1]—Adele Rogers St. John

Aging shuts down a variety of strenuous activities:
  • too old to ride bulls in rodeos
  • too old to be an assault ranger in the military
  • too old to safely test pilot a new Mach-3 jet
  • too old to be an NFL football running back

Ken Dychtwald's definitive *Age Wave* dealt with six common myths about seniors: that people over sixty-five are old; that most older people are in poor health; that older minds are not as bright as young minds; that older people are unproductive; that older people are unattractive and sexless; and that all older people are pretty much the same.[2]

There is also the myth that mature adults are not easily tempted. That seeming automatic perfection falls on Christian seniors is all smoke and mirrors. Robert South [1634-1716] challenged the assumption that aging guarantees moral improvement, "for sin never dies [with age]...the longer a blot continues the deeper it sinks....It is naturally impossible for an old man to grow young again; and it is next to impossible for a decrepit aged sinner to become a new creature and be born again [on his own]"[3]

Everyone, including mature adults, is pressured or tempted to do or go wrong. That's a biblical fact and a Christian "given." Conventional wisdom holds temptations disappear in retirement. But we should know better.

WHERE IS EVIL AFTER FIFTY?

Is the Devil left in a former workplace, or does Satan also tag along on tours and trips? When the body declines to kick up dust, does that mean Satan has vacated our space? Does evil evaporate from human nature past age sixty-five? Are appearances of calm proof of calm? Can't calm conceal hidden churning? Does inner turbulence automatically become harmless in our sixties? Are those seventy and eighty years of age more tranquil than in earlier decades? Does fuming cease in older adults? Are sinful attitudes absent? Do they dwindle, die, or disappear with age?

Sins *in* mature adults, not just sin *against* mature adults, has to be addressed. Many assume retirees aren't solicited to sin. But formidable temptations can waylay and whomp seniors!

Some think the only profligate behavior some elders indulge is budget-killing spending sprees. Or their sinning gets rationalized as "slippage." Lots of us are willing to dismiss acting up as outside the pale of wrongdoing. Individual repentance is no longer on seniors' agenda. At worst, seniors can lament their past mistakes rather than admit to present evil.

But mature adults are neither disease-proof nor sinproof. Longevity is not a safeguard against sinning, but can become the platform for more aggressive Satanic attacks.

The most neglected subject in senior years may be temptation. As we age, pains may become more diffused, aches more frequent, and recovery more prolonged. But temptations are not fewer, less persistent, less subtle, or less dangerous.

Is "Temptation" the Right Word?

Some would object to using the word "temptation" for any age. Some think this word is no longer suitable to explain human behavior. In many non-Christian circles, talk of temptation is regarded as pious drivel. Others think that to inject "temptation" into discussion introduces a mystical self-evaluation. Secular commentators view the concept of temptation to be a fictitious fog generated to keep guilt alive. Rather than speaking of attractions as temptations, they are supposed to be viewed as opportunities. Anton Levay, head of the Church of Satan, once described temptation as nothing more than motivation.

At the center of disdain for temptation is disdain for the Christian concept of sin. One can trace reduced awareness of temptation back to the reduction of what constitutes sin. "There are fewer temptations," claimed psychologist Wayne Oates, "because there are fewer sins."[4] Elimination of the word "temptation" is not the most grievous erasure, however. Etienne Gilson wrote, "the real trouble with our times is not the multiplication of sinners, it is the disappearance of sin."[5]

Christians, however, cannot give up the concept of temptation because we cannot give up the concept of sin. And we cannot give up the concept of sin without giving up the authority of Scripture as the self-revelation of the God who prescribes a moral law.

IS SATAN MADE A
SCAPEGOAT FOR OUR BEHAVIOR?

The real Devil's Triangle does not lie off Bermuda but is anywhere—wherever youth, middle-agers, and elders congregate. The real Devil's Triangle is not a geographical area in the ocean, but the interpersonal space in which the proverbial foes of Christian conduct are at work: the world, the flesh, and the Devil. Satan can snare us in traps that look harmless enough, as well as through more obvious worldly ploys. Those who deny the validity of temptation deny the reality of Satan. Some see Satan not as an actual being bent on disrupting Christian values, but as a speculative symbol devised by those who want to make sense out of rampant bad behavior and human destructiveness. Others consider Satan nothing more than a protagonist, a literary device, such as Mephistopheles in Goethe's *Faust*.

The late medieval view of Satan as a frightful goat-like monster renders a gross disservice to countless Christians. Today's Christian needs to realize that Satan's strategies more often are to charm, soothe, and compliment than to scare, scar, and savagely abuse. He is not a cosmic King Kong who chomps on characters like Judas

Iscariot. Rather, he approaches us more like a suave gentleman or a sweet lady, close counterfeits of Paul's "angels of light."

Scripture consistently presents Satan as a cosmic person in competition with God. The Devil is a debased angel with diabolical intentions. Just as there cannot be love without a lover, hatred without one who shows hate, or holiness without a Holy One, so there can be no devilishness without a devil.

> Many doubt Satan's existence and reality.
> Men don't believe in a devil now,
> As their fathers used to do;
> They have forced the door of the broadest creed
> To let his form pass through.
> There isn't a print of his cloven hoof,
> Or a fiery dart from his bow,
> To be found in earth or air today,
> For the world has voted so.
> But who is mixing the fatal draft,
> That palsies heart and brain?...
> Who dogs the steps of toiling saint,
> And digs a pit for his feet?
> Who sows the tares in the field of time
> Whenever God sows His wheat?
> The devil is voted not to be,
> And of course "the thing is true;"
> But who is doing the kind of work
> The devil alone could do?
>
> —Alfred J. Hough[6]

Jesus' temptation in the desert is reduced to an imaginary event if the Devil is not real. Moreover, Jesus' last triumph, intended to destroy the works of the Devil (1 John 3:8) is rendered a meaningless act if the Devil is not real. Jesus' intelligence is riddled with stupidity if Satan is merely a folk superstition. Since Jesus was the only one present in His wilderness temptations, He is our direct source about them. If there is no Satan, Jesus should have debunked recognition of Satan just as the Sadducees had done.

Evil and suffering are so very personal. Personal because we are attacked and pursued by a unique person who has devised temptations. Scripture accounts for our struggles through Satan's involvement. For millennia, proposed alternatives have denied or downplayed this personal character of evil.

Does Satan bother with retirees? Many think youths are more tempted than mature adults. A widely held view is that seniors dwell in the Land of Nod far removed from the street of Naughtiness. Youth seems to be temptation's Velcro. Retirement is its Teflon. Temptations *stick to* youth, but *slide off* retirees. Is that true?

> "When the devil grows old, he turns hermit."
> —A Swiss proverb[7]

If this proverb were true, temptations diminish and disappear with old age. But there is ample evidence that Satan does not turn his back on seniors. Both biblical seniors and living senior-saints come out of the twilight to tell of real battles to stay loyal to Christ. They testify that we misjudge Satan if we think he only frequents smoke-filled bars, air-wicked brothels, and sanitized gambling halls. Satan does not slight or consider lost causes those with white hair.

For starters, there is an age affinity that not even the Devil can shake off. After all, he is himself old—the old foe or ancient serpent (Rev. 12:9; 20:2). Another proof that seniors are important to him is that Satan has continued to try to make their lives miserable and get them to loiter on the sidelines where they lack the spiritual energy to do him further damage.

A person can sign on with Satan without knowing it. The prophet Ezekiel encountered old men who came to him claiming they were discipled, truly dedicated

(Ezekiel 14:1-4). In his commentary on that passage, Calvin noted that the elders pretended "a regard for piety when they had none."

Scripture makes the point that Satan's hatred for seasoned servants of Christ is intense and undying. So intense is his hatred for those who love Christ that Satan even orchestrates elaborate and expensive mockery of Christ's servants who are already dead (Rev. 11:8-10).

If you are a senior, don't pull up your spiritual oars to ease into quiet retirement, for the Devil is persistently paddling around your weathered bark looking for opportunities to capsize you. Satan circles everyone as he looks for strands of weakness. He delights to grab any loose ends, run with them, and unravel us. We are never too old to be tempted by the Devil.

The Jews of Jesus' day put themselves outside of Satan's empire (this view was challenged by Christ in John 8:44). A similar mistake is to presume that seniors are barricaded against Satan sowing his tares in their life.

Satan's temptations with seniors are strong enough to deflect their attention away from Christ, strong enough to discourage their continuance in Christ's church, strong enough to wreck their peace of mind, to reverse their spiritual growth, to diminish their Christian testimony, strong enough to weaken their ability to bounce back from trials, strong enough to throw them off balance and make them fall for scams they once saw through.

WHY ARE SENIORS TARGETED BY SATAN?

Anything slow is an easy target. On the other hand, speed has nothing to do with our vulnerability to temptation. Our state of our minds, rather than the condition of our bodies, has everything to do with temptation's power.

In 1964, my wife, Roberta, and I enjoyed Richard Burton's [1925-1984] Broadway stage performance of *Hamlet*. I had never witnessed such intensity and cunning in the Hamlet character. Burton's mastery was riveting and electrifying. His talents so impressed his fellow-actor Hume Cronyn that he was convinced Burton was touched by the finger of God as few are.[8] Off stage Burton and Elizabeth Taylor lived together though both were married to others. In his last decade Richard Burton confessed, "As one gets older [the Devil] invades your mind through all kinds of channels."[9]

But age is relative. Also known for his infidelities, French poet, novelist, and playwright Victor Hugo [1802-1865], whose last great work was written at eighty-one, saw youth in age and age in youth. He said, "Forty is the old age of youth; fifty is the youth of old age."

At twenty-seven, Scottish essayist Robert Louis Stevenson [1850-1894] saw in seniors frailties peculiar to their years. He wrote in his essay, "Crabbed Age and Youth":

> Old people have faults of their own; they tend to become cowardly, niggardly, and suspicious. Whether from the growth of experience or the decline of animal heat, I see that age leads to these and certain other faults.[10]

Vulnerability to temptation varies from person to person, of course. But temptations change as we age. Martin Luther [1483-1546] knew a lot about the Devil's cleverness and cunning. Once around his meal table Luther warned students to watch out for Satan's diversity. In May, 1532, Luther commented on how temptations change with age.

> Young fellows are tempted by girls, men who are thirty years old are tempted by gold, when they are forty

years old they are tempted by honor and glory, and those who are sixty years old say to themselves, 'What a pious man I have become!'[11]

Because character formation goes on even as we age, why shouldn't the Devil keep oldsters in his sights? After all, what greater success could he claim than to bamboozle, hoodwink, and capture a creaky soldier of the cross?

Satan is no respecter of age. Every age level feels his attack. Satan works overtime to ruin our spiritual tranquillity whether we are fifteen or fifty. Forever anti-Christ, he seeks to lessen Christ in us. Where Christ is most present and pronounced, there Satan feels most challenged to beat godly defenses. A working Christ enrages Satan. And mature adults who know Christ best can expect the worst abuse Satan can conceive.

Do Temptations Lessen in Time?

One way to beat the Devil at his game is to expose his tactics. And one way that helps us do that is to specify those "certain other faults" Stevenson alluded to. While some temptations may diminish in later years, others diversify, intensify, and mystify. Temptations do not bubble up like natural springs, borne only on a flood of powerful hormones. More often, temptations creep over seniors in the blindfolds of indifference and blankets of moodiness.

Physical changes accompany aging. When a person becomes frail and fragile, some "old" temptations fizzle. The body wears down.

> Deterioration of the various parts of the body proceeds at different rates of change and generally is so slow that it cannot be measured as accurately at weekly, monthly, or even annual intervals. Not all indications of age appear with equal severity in a given individual.[12]

First, let's distinguish between senescence and senility. Younger people too often equate senescence with senility. *Senescence* is normal body slowdown. *Senility*, however, is an abnormal mental condition in the elderly.

Senescence does not necessarily lead to senility. The loss of bodily powers does not mean we cease to be mentally alert and agile. If bodily decline, including death, is a consequence of Satan's desire to disrupt the functioning of God-given life, demoralization, discouragement, and depression among many seniors are tools in Satan's overall strategy.

WHAT ABOUT SEX FOR SENIORS?

Aging does result in some faculty limitations and slowdown. When we get into our seventies and eighties, it can seem that nature has closed off whole wings of temptation. So what damage can Satan do with what is left?

Mature adults continue to be sexually active, but in varying degrees. In aging, sexual activity usually slows.[13] Most past sixty are less prone to be sexually promiscuous compared to middle-agers, for example.

> After going through six stages in man, humans come to the last stage, "second childishness, and mere oblivion, *sans* [French for "without"] teeth, sans eyes, sans taste, sans everything!"—Shakespeare, *As You Like It.*

If seniors go over to the Devil, for the most part it is not down alleys of sleaze. A ninety-year-old man once bragged of his alleged sexual potency. A reporter asked him, "How would you like to die?" True to form, he responded, "I'd like to be killed by her angry suitor." Few seniors, however, imagine they are carnal bait. They are content to be a trophy "Dear" to the one they married. Thoughts of adulterous liaisons have a short life, at best. Such an evil does not sign us up on Satan's team unless that imagination is kept, nurtured—even obeyed.

Romantic love, however, does not die at seventy. At seventy-three, Elton Trueblood wrote the following playful limerick for his wife Virginia:

> My wife is a fabulous beauty,
> And even in age she's a cutey;
> She sits in the sun,
> And thinks it is fun,
> To be far, far away from her duty.[14]

Luther cited an old medieval saying that temptations are like birds circling overhead. They become sin only when they nest in our heads. But sometimes temptations never get airborne! A persistent desire for a wild fling cannot evolve into genuine temptation when physical ability to consummate the contemplation has departed. Strangely, but surely, in this instance the compulsive thought can be sinful without it becoming a fulfilled temptation.

The tempter crafts seductions to any individual. His tactics are especially subtle for seasoned Christians. He pits his expertise against ours. We can be out-matched and out-maneuvered. Seniors have a lot to fear—and learn—from the master of deceit.

How Do Jesus' Temptations Relate to Ours?

Christ's confrontation with Satan in the wilderness continues to be the Christian paradigm for understanding Satan's *modus operandi*. According to Matthew, the temptation of old man Moses anticipated the temptation of young man Jesus. Jesus near the *start* of His career and Moses near the *end* of his career were both assaulted by Satan.

Jesus was His own man, not a Moses double. For one thing, Jesus refused to repeat the manna miracle. Yet some similarities show a theological dynamism at work. Earlier, Matthew's account drew a parallel between Jesus' coming out of Egypt and the Jewish Exodus (Matt. 2:15). Jesus was the New Moses destined to effect a New Exodus. That Jesus used Moses' answers to Israel from Deuteronomy 6-8 showed that Jesus was a prophet much like Moses. Jesus used Moses to mop up Satan when he cited Moses to answer the Devil.

A symbolic tie stretched backward and forward. Moses was hounded by Israel at first for forty days and later for over forty years. Imagine facing complaints for forty *years*! Jesus fit the Mosaic model by being harassed by Satan forty *days*. One inference from this was that Satan could compress his pressure to days rather than spreading it out. Though greater than Moses, Jesus was not above Moses in facing temptation. Both men were at junctures where wrong decisions would have nose-dived their roles. Israel, "in an attitude of homicidal fury,"[15] charged Moses with cruelty for having brought them out of Egypt to apparently perish by starvation (Ex. 17:1-7).

Israel's put-down question—"Is the Lord among us or not?" (Ex. 17:7)—was a facsimile of Satan's sarcastic question— "If you are the Son of God, tell these stones to become bread" (Matt. 4:3).

For Jesus to hear the voice of Satan in the words of ancient Israel counters the charge that belief in the Devil was derived from Zorastrianism (Persian dualism). Behind the murmuring of Israel was the mad, malevolent Devil. Without going into details, the Bible's doctrine of Satan is radically different, at once more sophisticated, yet simpler, than pagan dualism—which divides the visible world between naturally evil and good parts.

In the first temptation, Satan suggested Jesus was

stupid to allow himself to die of starvation. Jesus used Moses' reply to bickering Israel (Deut. 8:1-4) when He refused to use His miracle power to save His own skin. Jesus was attacked to prevent His mission. Moses was attacked in the midst of fulfilling his mission. Ironically, He who was greater than Moses emulated Moses but in a higher capacity (Heb. 2:18-5:8). Jesus fasted as did Moses; like Moses (Ex. 34:28), Jesus fasted forty full days and nights (Matt. 4:2).

Why did Moses fast? Why did Jesus fast? For the same reason Moses fasted. Neither was overweight. For both men Israel was, though blessed by God, distant from God. Their fasting was incidental to praying. Moses' fast was the precedent for our Lord's experience in the wilderness. Moses' fast was part of his intercession for the people (Deut. 9:9, 18, 25). In order to disrupt their praying, Satan's attack on both was to divert, dilute, and deflect their mission objectives, which for Moses was to receive the Law and, for Jesus, to establish the Gospel.

But there is another rarely noticed feature of Satan's sly temptation. He was tempting Jesus to "serve me *now*! Live in immediate gratification. Become my captive in the prison of the present." The way he still tempts us to "get it all *now*." Jesus did not fall for the "show me the money" approach to success because the Father had guaranteed the kingdoms of the world to Him.

Satan still attacks young and old to impede their spiritual growth. He wants everyone thrown off track. His chief delight is to distort our perspectives and get us to live without spiritual direction.

In the following chapters, fourteen temptations common to senior Christians are considered. Not everyone will agree with their citations. Some will question my list on grounds that every one of these temptations meet people throughout life. Teenagers, for instance, can be as gossipy as some grannies. If these temptations trap us

as seniors, chances are good that they were poorly
resisted in earlier years. We just don't pass sixty and
then, all of a sudden, get bombarded with brand new
temptations. Nor would I suggest that these temptations are equally powerful with all seniors. Rather, I'm
proposing that some of aging's hazards can reignite old
temptations poorly handled in the past.

Our temptations are strong precisely because they
are old. Admittedly, for some of us, these temptations
already are a way of life. They may not be unfulfilled
temptations; they are established traits and routine reactions. Instead of being gimpy temptations, they are
genuinely ingrained faults.

We must want God to give us eyes to see how His
grace can make temptations less defiling and damaging! The bottom line for senior spirituality is greater
reliance on the Holy Spirit and a fuller commitment to
Christ. Our adherence to Christ in the thick of temptations is not something which arises from our own power
(1 Cor. 10:12).

> No temptation is too strong to be resisted with the help
> of divine grace. The tempter's power is but that of a
> fallen creature. God's power is always present to bring
> us through the darkest and most oppressive tunnel of
> temptation to the brighter sunlight of victory.[16]

WINNING WAYS

- When the years go *up*, temptations do not go *down*. We never outgrow the tendency toward wrongdoing. This admission forewarns us to seek Christ.

- Of course, seniors would be saved *from* temptation if there were no Devil. But Scripture tells us of evil without and evil within. We can be saved *in* temptation. Christ delivers us from evil as we depend on Him.

- Temptations begin as evil thoughts. Let our minds be saturated with Scripture. "Lean not unto your own understanding" (Prov. 3:5, KJV).

- Camphor fumes chase moths from our closets. Christ in His Word, like a camphor insect repellent, is pungent. His Word can chase non-Christian myths and preserve us from the gnawing destructive action of temptations. "Temptations lose their power when God is near."

∼ NOTES ∼

2

TEMPTED TO
WITHDRAW

I don't believe in retirement. For me or anyone else.... If
I thought retirement was a good move, would I still be
working at the age of ninety-five? I could have retired
thirty years ago. So it's not as though I haven't had time
to change my mind.[1]—George Burns

Mental flexibility encourages a spirit of openness and
growth in old age, while mental rigidity seems to be
associated with intellectual stagnation and eventual
withdrawal.[2] —William M. Clements

Trace the commendable rarely-miss patterns of adult
church attendance to their origin. What do we find? In
most cases, lifelong church attendance goes back to
childhood. By habits acquired in youth and practiced
through the years, church has become a second home, a
refuge when weary and a place of happy memories.

When I started in the ministry, I was somewhat
alarmed at the substantial percentage of those in the
membership over age fifty-five. It wasn't long before I
realized that those faithful seniors were the congregation's backbone.

Many churches depend heavily upon members over fifty. Indeed, without volunteer and financial support from godly seniors, many Christian causes would crumble. Although their physical health varies, many godly seniors demonstrate remarkable spiritual vitality and financial generosity, keeping churches strong.

Faithful church attendance is high among those seniors, not only in Florida and Arizona (where retiree populations are proportionately higher than in other states), but in some of the coldest regions of the nation.

I heard of an adult program on Thursday mornings at the Canton, Ohio, Baptist Temple that in ten years went from 54 in attendance to an average attendance of 800, and a high of over 2,261. Obviously, with that many seniors they could form a new congregation. But they are glad to contribute to the larger body by being one of its vital branches.

Who holds the longest church attendance records? Few have carried forward the injunction of the Apostle Paul about seniors being a good example to younger believers better than woman from the Nashville, Tennessee area. A local newspaper paid tribute to her for the 1,040 consecutive Sunday attendance record she set. Mrs. Craig was in her eighties at the time. Nashville citizens were reminded that there was something more to life than the Grand Ole Opry.

As I recall, church members wondered what was the matter with Mrs. Craig? Didn't it ever rain or snow in her town on Sundays or didn't she ever get unexpected company? Didn't she go anywhere Saturday nights so that she was too tired to attend Sunday worship services? Didn't she ever become angry at the minister or have her feelings hurt by someone and feel justified in staying home? Didn't she feel that she could worship just as well at home watching a preacher on TV while she gets her ironing done? What in the world is the matter with Mrs. Craig anyway?[3]

Surveys show that women attend church more than men. Why? It may be due in part to the fact that more women survive their husbands. Other reasons may be that women tend to be more socially oriented, more intellectually interested, and more spiritually committed than most men.

Simone de Beauvoir saw old men as loners. She added, "Old women have more shared interests and therefore more subjects for agreement and disagreement."[4]

Regional patterns on male vs. female church participation vary. It is sad that some seniors give up going to church. Sadder still is the fact that most parishioners do not miss them or tell them that they are missed.

Let's not eulogize the single stage for seniors. Surveyed spouses have demonstrated marvelous coping abilities; life is harder—not easier—alone. One cannot avoid temptations by retreating either from the church or from the world. Jesus' temptations show that Satan will not cease to pester us when we stop going out.

Seniors who pull way from societal interaction only paint themselves into a corner. Solitude can energize revolutionaries, but seniors' self-ostracizing is destructive. Satan's aim, in part, is to increase our decline by cutting us off from healthy contact with the outside world, especially with other Christians.

No biblical basis can justify becoming a senior hermit. One cannot defend seclusion as Christian because Jesus was led by the Holy Spirit into the wilderness. If that were true, Adam's Eden-hiding from God was smart (Gen. 3:8). Just as it was unwise for Adam to withdraw into a thicket, it is foolish for Christian seniors to lock the door against involvement.

VARIOUS KINDS OF WITHDRAWAL

Mark 1:12 deliberately placed Jesus' baptism so close to Jesus' wilderness temptation. How, then, does one explain this withdrawal following His baptism? Was it a temporary disappearance to deepen devotion or an unhealthy retreat into self-centeredness? The word "immediately" described the connection between the *high* of His baptism and the *low* of His temptation.

Both Jesus and Satan found solitude conducive to concentration. Later, Jesus would not give up the practice of seeking privacy just because the first time He tried it He was confronted by the Devil. Jesus continued to withdraw to pray (Luke 6:12). His prayer retreat did not signal an endorsement to withdraw from society because He returned to his mission renewed and refreshed. His times of solitude had a purpose, a high mission intention. And, that has been true of major leaders' brief exiles throughout history.

Jesus' exiles often were at night following a full day of work (Mark 1:35-39; 6:45f; 14:26-42). He didn't have a fixation about where He would and would not retreat. He chose different places to meditate (Tyre and Sidon [Mk.7:24]; Border of Decapolis [Mk. 7:31]; Dalmanutah in Southwest Galilee [Mk. 8:10]; Bethsaida east [Mk. 8:22]; Caesarae Phillipi [Mk. 8:27]; Perea [Jn. 10:40-11:54]). For Him withdrawal was a help and refreshment, not a crutch; a shelter, not a holiday. In Hebrew culture the persecuted would often pull back to let volatile situations cool and to avoid lethal clashes (Ps. 59:16; Jn. 11:54; 12:36; 18:2).

When Jesus drew apart, He did not suggest abandoning contact with the world. He was in the world, not of it. He pulled aside to pray and to revitalize His prophetic energy. Dietrich Bonhoeffer [1906-1945] admitted the difficulty of bringing a sharp witness to a world bent on dulling our spiritual edge. He outlined the rationale of periodic Christian retreats in his now-famous work, *Life Together.*

Unlike the Jewish Essenes, Jesus lived among people of differing views. Later Christian monasticism was an honest attempt to spare Christianity from pagan influences. Christian monasticism arose, in part, to correct forced participation in Rome's pagan rites.[5] Yet Jesus' disciples did not practice seclusion. Like the disciples, those past sixty should fight the urge to curl up in one's own corner.

SENIOR DROP-OUTS

When a person resigns the workplace, he or she retires. Early retirement—when unwanted—can be cruel and leaves some folks cynical, bitter, and depressed. But if one eyes a second occupation and new career, the joy of living can return. Some respite between careers can do wonders to rejuvenate. Benjamin Hooks, NAACP executive director, retired from that position at sixty-seven. Before he would consider a new challenge, he wisely wanted a little time off. He said, "I'd like to smell a few [flowers] before I start pushing them up."[6]

Fear puts some seniors in reverse when it comes to social involvement. One reason is our fear of rejection. They see the signs of aging and believe they will be snubbed because of it. Job felt like an outcast (Job 31:33, 34). So did the psalmist: "Do not cast me away when I am old, do not forsake me when my strength is gone" (71:9, NIV). Age discrimination unfortunately sidelines many useful, talented, and willing retirees. One way we defend year-round hibernation is: "It is better to dodge neglect than to feel neglected." But it is obvious that detachment shortens life and engagement lengthens it.

Nationwide church attendance after age sixty shows a significant drop.[7] In large churches, packed pews, busy hallways, crowded doorways, and full aisles of strangers confuse and turn off some seniors. What we can't control, we can't tolerate. Our involvement depends on our openness to new experiences. Without physical closeness, one-on-one contact makes new relationships troublesome.

Initial awkwardness can be overcome. If you dislike large groups, challenge your own reaction. Fight the odds and obstacles and continue your church contacts so you can find social as well as spiritual enrichment.

Some might assume that diminished desire and energy after age sixty makes disengagement an attractive temptation. However, any declining physical powers should not tempt us to abandon our emotional investments in Christian community.

Salvation Army Brigadier Mary Bunton first retired at sixty-five, but she got bored in retirement. "I wouldn't have been happy staying home and doing nothing worthwhile." So she reenlisted in the Salvation Army and worked three days a week as a secretary at the Army's Adult Rehabilitation Center in Norwood, Ohio. After thirty more years at that job, she finally felt she should retire at ninety-five. She said, "I'm an ordinary person, but I have a wonderful God."[8]

Others drop out. Sociologist George M. Logan queried thirty thousand elderly persons on this question. Result: "more than half reported attending church less frequently than they did ten years ago. Transportation difficulties and low income combined with social pressure for financial support of the churches have offset attendance."

Donald Grey Barnhouse [1895-1960], pastor of Philadelphia's Tenth Presbyterian Church, wrote in his Sunday church bulletin:

> Let the elderly people of Philadelphia (and the impecunious student!) know that they are welcome here even

if they are not able to put a penny in the offering. In fact, if there is anyone who would like to come to church but who feels that they [sic.] cannot because of transportation difficulties, we would be glad to see that they [sic.] got street car tokens to bring them. The church is here to serve those in need.

Financially solvent retirees may find Logan's research difficult to appreciate. But in the early 1960s two social scientists collaborated in surveying elderly non-church goers and they came up with similar findings. Those were:

- they feel pushed aside
- they can't contribute financially
- they are unable to dress well
- they feel they look old, even ugly.[9]

Why should physical appearance discourage church involvement? God does not look on the outward appearance, but upon the heart (1 Samuel 16:7). Age is "that ill layer up of beauty" (*Henry V*). A tattered coat can be mended, but textured skin is permanent. David didn't need a clear mirror to see that his skin was shriveled like a wineskin in a smoke house (Ps. 119:83). When one's face is lined as finely and deeply as a map of the Tour de France, self-worth often suffers. De-emphasizing facial creases can be a challenge and an art. Kathrine Hepburn's face is heavily wrinkled, but she dismisses her leathery-looking skin. Do your best to look your best, and look forward to the final makeover in eternity.

The new bodies of Christians in resurrection will be without skin wrinkles. Christ will present us in our final state "a radiant church, without stain or wrinkle [of age, lit. Greek] or any other blemish" (Eph. 5:27, NIV).

DISENGAGEMENT IMPULSES

Some feel protected by noninvolvement. The temptation to disengage is a step beyond the temptation to withdraw because it is more permanent. But disengagement is less likely when we are convinced we have something to contribute. Withdrawal in our sixties and early seventies is a conscious choice, not an unavoidable condition. Regretably, a significant number of seniors lose their incentive to fight bodily ills and thus cease church activities. Reasons for self-chosen social isolation range from loss of mate, loss of sight, loss of hearing, and loss of mobility to fear of rejection.

Deliberate neglect of the assembly of worshipping saints is instigated by negative forces, for Christians of all ages are urged not to neglect their assembly (Heb. 10:25, 39). To justify missing church by saying, "it is too much trouble" sanctions gnawing emptiness and tempts one to more damaging self-centeredness—the essence of sin.

How to Avoid Disengagement

How can desire for isolation be overcome? Above all, avoid those mental cutoffs that precede and produce disengagement. Withdrawal is an extension of withholding. Withdrawal and withholding often are subtle forms of fear, anger, retaliation, and spite. Simone de Beauvoir gave examples of how that happens, saying that total separation is secretly sought to spare seniors more agony.

> [Old people] often withdraw...[or] 'un-commit' themselves [to] cut off their emotional relationships with others. They feel the need for this all the more since they are emotionally vulnerable.[10]

All of us have overheard complaints in churches about so-and-so being unfriendly or being snubbed. In such circumstances, we can identify with Ezekiel's description of "malicious neighbors who are painful briers and sharp thorns" (28:24, NIV). Avoidance of back-stabbing neighbors can be wise. But what happens when a church becomes a collection of thorny shrubs? A prime excuse for avoiding church is this: Why go to a place where hurts increase?

Seniors don't want to be pampered and overprotected, but neither do we want to be slighted, ignored, and made to feel unwanted. Overconcern for propriety can create a deadly chill in churches. It is when churches are warm, welcoming, accepting, and friendly that seniors find an atmosphere to our liking.

Coming to a church where Scripture is honored, where its message is faithfully preached and taught, builds up faith and injects buoyancy for smoother sailing through our latter days. Separation from the company of fellow Christians weakens our resistance to other temptations. In contrast, participation in the company of fellow Christians strengthens our resistance to infections and disease. A recent Duke University scientific study of more than seventeen hundred adults sixty-five and over in North Carolina found that once-a-week church attendance has produced a healthy influence on the immune system. Dr. Harold Koenig, director of Duke's Center for the Study of Religion/Spirituality and Health, published these findings in the October, 1997 issue of the *International Journal of Psychiatry in Medicine*.

In contrast to previous studies based on personal interviews, the new study measured blood samples for levels of interleukin 6 and other substances that regulate immune and inflammatory responses. It was found that "those who attended religious services once a week were about half as likely as non-attenders to have elevated levels of IL6." Usually, high IL6 is associated with stress and depression. Lower IL6 levels point to an immunity benefit from participation in religious services.[11]

Pulling away from younger members only compounds mental aging. Going it alone allows bitter feelings to develop. Seclusion leads to further aggravations and vexations. Martin Luther urged those who wanted to cut back and cease church involvement to flock together continually.

Drawing aside is no solution to anxiety, hurt, and frustration. Withdrawal impoverishes us. Privacy does not reduce temptations but allows them to become more powerful. In isolation our values may not collapse, but they become distorted, shallow, and self-centered. Living apart from the company of fellow Christians fosters stagnation and spiritual sterility.

WHY CHRISTIAN SENIORS
SHOULD STAY ACTIVE

Satan was glad to have a go at Jesus in His prime. Many of us can identify with Jesus' facing a free fall from the top of the Temple roof. Heights are naturally threatening at any age. The promise of an angel catch had all the promise of a secure bungee chord attached to a stationary platform. But, Satan's favorite places to inflict temptations are on *terra ferma,* in lulls, low spots, and emotional valleys.

Jesus loves us to the end (John 13:1). That means God does not disengage from us when we grow old. Our grip may slacken its former strength, but God holds us firmly in His hand (John 10:28). God's grip on us in Christ not even the Devil can unclasp. And the Lord, who does not let us go, wants us in Christian worship and work.

The Holy Spirit does not lead us into fruitless isolation, but deeper into family life, into Christian fellowship, and deeper into Bible studies. It is refreshing to read of eighty-year-old Marion Munger of Jackson, Mississippi, who retired from teaching after fifty-six years, yet who delights to share in small groups the fruits of early morning Bible study. She said:

> People who just put their feet up and rest in retirement miss so much! God intends for us to enrich each others' lives. We all gain through our heartbreaks and failures; how can we hold onto that and never do any good with it? The diamonds and rubies from God's Word surface only as you grow older. As they do, you should want to share them with others. If we help each other, we create a stronger church and a stronger America.[12]

The Spirit wants to increase our skills in prayer and in understanding God's Word. But we cannot grow in Christ if we are bent on "advancing to the rear."

Kick the blues by convincing yourself that God wants you in His work in some capacity. Involvement, not withdrawal, is what you need. You can still contribute. A group of senior citizens in St. Cloud, Minnesota, dropped the phrase "Senior Citizens" to describe their group. They now call themselves "The Chronologically Gifted." I once spoke to a group of Kentucky seniors who called themselves "The JOY Club." I asked what "joy" stood for, and they replied with beaming faces "Just Older Youth."

> Make friends of God's children,
> Help those who are weak; Forgetting in nothing,
> His blessings to seek.
> [W. D. Longstaff; G.C. Stebbins]

> Charles H. Spurgeon [1834-1892] at age forty-three said, "Have not many aged persons a gentleness and an impressiveness which peculiarly qualify them to arrest the attention of the young? As they know more by experience than most of us, should they not be all the readier to impart instruction? It was always my delight to sit at my grandfather's feet when he told of his experiences of the grace of God. When he was eighty years old or more his witness to the faithfulness of God

was worth going many miles to hear. If you dislike large groups, challenge your own reaction. Fight the odds and obstacles and continue your church contacts so you can find social and spiritual enrichment. There are scores of aged men and women whose life story ought to be often told among children, with their loving ways and cheerful manners. They would be an acquisition to any school for the children's sake while to the teachers their weight and wisdom would be an incalculable benefit. Die in harness, my brethren, if your mental and physical vigor will permit." (*Metropolitan Tabernacle Pulpit*, Vol. 23:629f.)

Dr. Francis Otto Schmitt, professor of molecular biology at MIT, was honored on his 70th birthday with a dinner. When asked about retirement, he said, "There are two meanings of this word, and to me, 'retire' means to put new tires on the old chassis and get going again."[13]

Social historians wisely write up—not off—senior capabilities and achievements in art and literature. From antiquity, elders have applied significant insights and talents, making major contributions to the welfare of their culture and times. Their retirement years were not chewed up by aimless diversions, endless hobbies, and nonstop travel.

You can do much for Christ in your mature years. Get in touch with others by being a caregiver, a teacher, or take an active role in a mentoring program to get back on the path of service.

Sir George Williams [1821-1905], while a young British merchant, founded the YMCA (Young Men's Christian Association) in 1844. The first Association in the United States, commemorated by a tablet at Central Congregational Church in Boston, was founded December 29, 1851. More significant than the age of its founder, more enduring than the Y's sturdy gymnasiums was his Christian commitment. The YMCA began as a Christian ministry, with Bible studies and evangelistic programs. Its first Declaration of the Association had as its purpose: "uniting those young men who, regarding Jesus Christ as their God and Savior according to the Holy Scriptures, desire to be His disciples in their doctrine and in their life."[14]

At eighty-three, Sir Williams was still active in the organization, inspiring fellow workers to keep its evangelical torch burning. At their golden wedding anniversary celebration in 1905, Sir Williams publicly reflected on life with his wife and his ministry with the YMCA. He spoke enthusiastically about his continued contribution.

According to his biographer—"his face lit up, he faced the future, saying that he hoped he would be spared some years to come. The old warrior would not lay by his armor while he had strength to bear it. He had long passed the allotted span of a man's life, but there was fight in him still. 'So long as I have any strength left,' he said, 'I will fight. There is still much to be done. God helping me, I will fight the Evil One to the end.'"[15]

Fine words! A flashing witness, too. But it was not pious rhetoric, for Sir Williams engaged himself in personal witness even outside the confines of the YMCA.

> [Into his eighties] every Sunday afternoon you might have met him in the neighborhood of Russell Square, his hands full of [Gospel] tracts which he distributed with a kindly word to the passersby, stopping now and again to speak to some cabmen on the rank or to address a word of Gospel invitation to a street loafer.[16]

Like John the Baptist, George Williams was a burning and shining light. Christians cannot burn brightly for Christ unless their witness wicks are well-trimmed and their spiritual fuel is daily replenished. Those growing in Christ must be involved with fellow Christians. As our own spiritual energy is replenished and increased, we can use more of it to help others become stronger, more involved Christians.

WINNING WAYS

• Stepping out can be as difficult as stepping up. But reading about Christ's lively stride into His society helps us to regain our moral balance, motivate our social conscience, and guide our spiritual direction.

• To step out with Christ is a step closer to holiness. Forget status shoes for service. Put on the sturdy shoes of the Gospel of peace, for then we can minister in meekness and with mercy.

• When we lack transportation to worship with the family of God, don't be hesitant to ask for a ride. What are friends for? Churches promote body life and should be vitally interested in the recruitment and involvement of mature adults.

• More and more churches have handicap parking, hearing enhancement devices in the pews, wheelchair ramps, passenger vans, elevators, and electrical chair lifts—all open invitations for involvement for those with varying degrees of disability.

THINGS TO THINK ABOUT—

[1] Distinguish between solitude, seclusion, and separation. Give examples. Is it evil to want to have private time?

[2] Can retreats encourage reclusiveness? Can Christians invest in others without personal involvement?

[3] Many seniors have successfully turned to writing. Begin with the New Testament writer Paul. Paul eventually called himself "an old man" (Phil. 5:9 NIV). He wrote five significant and outstanding letters in his last years: Colossians, Philemon, Titus, 1 and 2 Timothy. But the crowning literary contributor to the New Testament canon was that seraphic ancient, the apostle John. According to many scholars, he wrote the last five New Testament books. What were they? (name them)

[4] Octogenarian Denver Seminary Chancellor Dr. Vernon Grounds wrote: "How crucial it is...for our churches to develop cadres of caregivers who understand the needs of older members and give them not only concrete helpfulness but also, and even more importantly, attention, gratitude, respect and patient love." (*Focal Point*, Spring, 1995, p. 6). What has your church done to attract seniors, involve, and evangelize them?

[5] How can retirees be involved in our church without seeming to be pushy? How can our church programs better promote greater senior involvement? Have our church boards ever addressed this need?

∼ NOTES ∼

3

TEMPTED TO BE BOSSY

---○---

For some old people, to give advice, to tell other people
what they ought to do, is a way of getting revenge for
being deprived of the opportunity of direct action.[1]
                                           —Paul Tournier, M.D.

Bossiness a temptation? How can bossiness be a temptation when bossiness is obviously rude, insensitive, and
repulsive?

Bossiness hides itself in demanding attention and,
strangely, in some compassionate intervention and caregiving. Its unattractive side appears in Shakespeare's
King Lear, who badgered his daughters for their failure
to flatter him.

Many miss subtle bossiness because it is not always
obvious. We meet it less as furious, brutal demands and
more in the form of placid, compliant, even gracious
delegating. And can it not be found in the urge to
"advise"? (The word advise often replaces the word
"admonish.") Anyone who says they want to help may
not realize that his or her volunteerism can be a disguise
for an unrecognized tyrannical impulse. The chief reason why bossiness can be a temptation is its ability to
disguise itself as a good thing.

Bossiness lurks beneath fussiness. When a person refuses to conform, it is the boss in him that objects and outlaws. Refusing to eat, refusing to cooperate, even refusing to live can become forms of bossiness— just as withdrawal may indicate that we don't like to be pushed.

Can anyone escape *being* bossed? We find ourselves bossed by diseases, by medical dependence, and by organized events that interrupt our routines or preferences.

Are those over fifty any bossier than other folks? Merely to suggest that seniors are domineering and dictatorial is sure to get some folks' dander up. Let's step back and be objective while we sort through the varieties of supervision.

ARE RETIREES NATURALLY BOSSY?

Evidence seems to point the other way. Many surveys of attitudes among mature adults have been done. Several of these surveys showed that many seniors were distressed with loss of control in their churches. Here are some sample quotes: "Older people get squeezed out of their positions in church." Another said that "seniors get pushed out of their jobs at church." We've all heard similar venting of senior vexations.

When hints are dropped that a senior should resign or retire from a church post, a new hurt results. Some churches have suffered because qualified new members rarely appear in leadership positions. Be fair and realistic. Seniors no longer in elected office can engage in less visible but vital roles, still contributing to their church's life, programs, and future.

Church bylaws do their best to outlaw oligarchy, prevent domination, and neutralize controlling people who crave power to run everything. When does the expression "my church" cease to be neutral and signal a compulsive desire to dominate? Younger members feel defeated and drained of incentive to support their church when elected leaders are unresponsive, exclusive, and resistant to change. Older adults can discourage and, therefore, indirectly drive younger members from active leadership.

One of the proofs of true leadership is how effective we are in enlisting others to expand—and share—the range of responsibility in our church, no less than in the business world. To balk at the development of more leaders is a signal of latent bossism. Beware lest controlling leadership degenerates into rule and ruin. The church's leader is the Lord, not stand-in bosses.

A vital church shuns both anarchy and tyranny. Equality without balances can lead to control-by-clique, which can, in turn, lead to tyranny or its reverse: anarchy. "The church is not a 'holy autocracy.' It is the fellowship of believers who follow the one Lord and have been laid hold of by the one Spirit."[2] In the long run, it is far better to achieve power with people than to flex power over people.

BOSSING IS NOT INTRINSICALLY EVIL

All jobs require supervision. Without authority to regulate, govern, channel, and decide throughout the range from design to distribution, industry would be chaotic.

Bossing is not the same as bossiness. There is professional bossing and pejorative bossiness. To supervise is to boss, yet to flaunt one's supervisory role of supervision is to be bossy. Meddling is unwanted and unsolicited bossing, borderline bossiness. Whereas Scripture is pro-management, it is anti-bossism.

Many children accuse their parents of being bossy when they insist that they clean up their rooms. Is asking for order wrong? To accuse a parent of being unreasonable for requiring cleanliness, caution, and care does not qualify as bossiness. Children may not like that they need supervision, guidance, and direction. St. Paul also wrote of deacons supervising their children (1 Tim. 3:12).

At first, parents begin as autocrats, then balance their role with more and more democracy. Ideally, letting go happens gradually, in increments. Children may resent, resist, or ridicule parental authority but, without astute exercise of that authority, more serious problems are bound to arise.

When Simone de Beauvoir was a girl, she resisted her mother's occasional meddling. Of her youth she wrote, "...the conflict that threatened to set me against my mother did not break out; but I was uneasily aware of its underlying presence."[3]

Questions arise over the duration and degree of supervision, not its need. Excessive oversight can be counter-productive, robbing children of self-respect. Parents find it hard to "let go" of control over their children. Supervision is hard to relinquish; but unless we appropriately "let go" that relinquishment, children don't develop self-management or learn to take responsibility.

Conversely, in our elder years the need for supervision may return. Some of us may get to the point where we can't decide what to eat, how to dress, and where to walk. Nursing aids are invaluable to spare such seniors from unnecessary injury. Trained help can watch over those in "second childhood." Supervision becomes a necessary safety mechanism for disoriented, dependent adults.

Bossy streaks occur most often in home settings. Do husbands and wives, adult parents and adult children get along with genuine mutual respect? Relentless supervision stifles incentive, smothers creativity, and sours relationships. Scripture contains numerous examples of destructive bossiness. One comes to mind about an Old Testament woman who refused to be bossed by her tyrannical husband and lived to tell about it. Queen Vashti refused to obey her husband, the king, to "display her beauty" (Esther 1:11, NIV) before the king's drunken guests (Esther 1:10-22).

DO SOME WOMEN GET BOSSIER WITH AGE?

> A significant proportion of...older women (average age, fifty-eight)...become more assertive, more likely to rate themselves fairly high on traits that had been considered masculine, to call themselves boss in the family, and to be strongly motivated to do something on their own, outside of the family sphere.[4]—Betty Friedan.

Open defiance is one way a wife can resist a domineering husband. To save themselves from unnecessary injury, some wives take matters into their own hands through the courts to get fair treatment. More commonly, other offended spouses cope by passive flight, a less obvious form of manipulation.

Infidelity sometimes becomes a way to retaliate against a spouse's perceived domination. When spouses cannot manipulate control, they may resort to passive regression; its most common form may be the "silent treatment."

Do aggressive mates qualify as bossy? A wife or husband may view taking control as a practical necessity. In one of my seminars on senior temptations, a housewife offered one explanation: "The reason why women seem bossier is because men become messier!"

Before we honor stereotypes, remember that what constitutes a "mess" is subject to individual interpretation. Conditioning and previously agreed upon standards must be factored in when determining what is messy. Neither men nor women should weave their compulsive orderliness into ropes for hanging.

Today's seniors should avoid attempts to manage adult children. It demeans. Consider David in the Old Testament. It seemed that in his seventies David stepped out of bounds within his family. He treated his adult son, Solomon, as though he were a schoolboy. Behind the little phrase "for which I have made provision" (1 Chron. 29:19)—the "lame duck king" tried to justify his supervision of Solomon. The probability is that David secured materials for the Temple construction in a patronizing way because of Solomon's perceived "inexperience."

Solomon, however, needed straight talk on moral affairs rather than advice on Temple construction. David's supervision in warehousing construction supplies fed Solomon's sense of inferiority. David implied that Solomon could not figure out where to get building materials on his own. That was demeaning. Solomon was a grown man and not helpless.

PRESSURING OTHERS IS BOSSINESS

Abrupt, curt demands come from anger and produce anger. They drive a wedge between those with whom we are trying to communicate. The hearer may do what is called for, but resent the tone, phrasing, timing, and manner of the request. Requests are polite; commands are harsh. Things go smoother when wishes are expressed as questions rather than barked out like orders. It is never too late to learn to appreciate the effectiveness of questions "will you please...?" or "may I suggest...?" in place of an iron-fisted ultimatum. It is tragic when seniors ignore the value of diplomacy.

Rude manners and mean looks turn a neutral atmosphere into a hostile battleground. Paul said "love is never rude" (1 Cor. 13:5, Moffatt, *Living Bible*). Bossiness by itself is not a temptation for bulldozing dispositions that are patently offensive. Requests can be made without sharp tones and rough-edged words. Subtle bossiness is smiling, smooth, gentle, disguised as helpfulness and constructive action.

Keeping adults dependent on us is usually motivated by self-gratification. We noted David's mistake with Solomon. David didn't try to charm Solomon; he charged his son. The aging king felt a sense of old-time power when he treated Solomon as helpless. But what he said and how he said it were uncalled for.

Have we ever been approached by a person who seems to want to be helpful when their "showing" us only reinforced feelings of dependence on them? It was a subtle way of getting us to imagine we cannot perform well without their input.

Wayne Oates carried this insight a step further.

A psychotherapeutic adage says, 'Run like mad when tempted to help!' A psychiatrist in Boston once told a group of us, 'If you feel like you have to help someone, stop first and reexamine your compulsion to help until you are no longer driven to do so. Then you are ready to combine wisdom with your help'...In terms of Christian moral theology, we should say that such helpfulness sins against the persons being helped....The need to help...is not a pure unadulterated need to serve others....It is generously contaminated with the fantasy of our all powerfulness, the desire to control even the smallest details of other people's lives. In the final analysis, the people we are trying to help become a means to foster the dependency of the willing ones and declare as helpless those who resist. Resistance, contrary to much psychological moralization, is not always bad. It may be a cry for freedom from us, the 'helper.'[5]

DO WE GET BOSSIER OR
SWEETER WITH AGE?

Do we become bossier when we shift into retirement? Are retirees less affected by up and down moods? If their troubles are milder, do their dispositions become more even? Do neighborhood children see them as mean, suspicious, and grouchy, or do they come across as happy, forgiving, and gentle individuals? Do added years make them mellow or bitter? Are they bossier or more agreeable? If one was pushy as a youth, does that mean that—when a senior—we're doomed to be domicile demagogues?

Psychiatrist Paul Tournier offered these reflections on senior mellowing:

> ...generally speaking, old people seem to be divided into two well-defined categories, with a few intermediate shades. There are wonderful old people, kind, sociable, radiant with peace. Troubles and difficulties only seem to make them grow still further in serenity. They make no claims, and it is a pleasure to see them and to help them. They are grateful, and even astonished, that things are done for them, and that they are still loved. They read, they improve their minds, they go for quiet walks, they are interested in everything, and are prepared to listen to anyone. And then there are awful old people, selfish, demanding, domineering, bitter. They are always grumbling, and criticizing everybody. If you go and see them, they upbraid you for not having come sooner; they misjudge your best intentions, and the conversation becomes a painful conflict....[6]

Old age is like a magnifying glass which can show up tendencies that have been there for a long time. These tendencies become more accentuated with each succeeding stage of life, although perhaps they may not have been so visible until now.

The quality of life improves with aging or deteriorates with aging, depending upon what qualities are built into it.[7]

Are we bossier or sweeter with age? It depends so much on our life-history, habits, and attitudes about "correction." Tragically, a school yard bully may re-emerge as a domineering adult. On the other hand, they may change as Jacob did. He began as a youthful cheat but ended his career as an magnanimous patriarch, a "prince with God." By the grace of God, there is hope for old grouches.

BLUFF BEHIND BOSSINESS

The biggest self-appointed boss was the world's biggest bluff! "Who was that?" you ask. Answer: Satan.

Whenever we feel overwhelmed, run over, and intimidated by people, think of how Jesus showed up Satan. Bravado is a transparent attempt at self-support for a sagging ego. (Although, fresh from his toasty domicile, he was probably quite a tease in the hot wilderness.) Braggarts have low self-images that they attempt to shore up by imposing outrageous demands upon the unsuspecting.

In the first chapter, we noted Satan was behind those bombastic accusations by Israel against Moses. They accused him of stupidity and cruelty in taking them out of Egypt and through the hazards of the desert where their food supply ran short and they had no water. Satan gave Moses a hard time. Through protests of the people, he raged hard against Moses, but Moses did not fall over. Later, Satan would try a similar bluff against Christ.

In the third desert temptation of Christ (Matt. 4:8), Satan claimed to have the nations of the world in his power. Satan strutted so confidently. But he confused power with authority, as Christ knew full well. Like all wannabe power-players, his ploys were self-centered and hence lacked legitimate authority.

Some might think Satan's claim was accurate, that he was actually able to give Jesus the nations of the world. Whatever your view on whether government is God-given, inherently evil, or redeemable, the point is that Jesus called Satan's bluff. Jesus did not attempt to enter into a debate with Satan on that issue of world governance. He didn't have to. World ownership was not the issue. The world is His Father's. Satan was not in line for its possession.

Psalm 2:8 made it plain that Jesus would acquire possession of the kingdoms of the world through His Father's willing donation. God the Father promised His Son: "Ask of me and I shall give you the nations for your inheritance." "The earth is the Lord's and the fullness thereof" (Ps. 24:1).

Jesus did not concede Satan was right or condone his claim. He viewed the promise of Satan as a clever ruse. Satan had no deeds to nations, no authority over humanity, no cosmic capital. Satan was bluffing Jesus. He was a hollow boss.

Satan tried to convince Jesus he was powerful and possessed the nations. But beneath his power-player veneer, the Tempter was a mere creature. Lucifer didn't want to show his limitations to Jesus. He posed as a seller, but had no proof for his alleged kingdom ownership. "[Satan's] offer...was fraudulent.... The Devil's offer was bogus. There are no kingdoms for him to bestow."[8]

A narcissistic person has an exaggerated sense of his own importance and is preoccupied with his unlimited success, power, and brilliance. That fit Satan to a T. Satan is narcissistic to the core. In his attempt at self-certification, Satan also showed himself to be the supreme neurotic. A neurotic seeks to neutralize the rank and role of superiors. Satan has a chronic inferiority complex. He posed as Mr. Big, but he was a groveling, spiteful pauper.

Satan's goal was to tempt Jesus to misuse His power for personal advantage. He tried to exploit Jesus. Satan made an opportunistic attempt to get Jesus to think He was dependent upon Satan to become Lord of the nations. It was a potent exploitation. But Jesus would not be bamboozled by that cosmic windbag.

Think again about Jesus in His own temptation. He knows what it's like for us! Focus on Christ's victory over Satan. But also think on the Devil's empty pomposity. That will help us see how those who boss others are out to bolster their sense of self-importance.

Have we ever felt deflated, inferior when a bossy person yanked on our bridle? When we go the extra mile down Patience Road, it is not a bad reflection on us, on our capabilities, on our competence. Rather it is a sad commentary on the person who needs to win, order, and dominate us.

To Boss or Not to Boss, That is the Question!

King Saul was not authoritarian in his youth, but he turned despotic in his last years. Something in his old age had turned him into a tyrant. He began "a modest, wholesome, and trusting young man," but in his old age he "became increasingly selfish, self-serving, self-trusting."[9] In the end, Saul's defensiveness made him destructive. He was unwilling to pass onto a younger man the rights and privileges of royalty. Near his end, however, he lamented his bullying, for he confessed, in one of the saddest confessions in the Bible, "I have played the fool" (1 Sam. 26:21).

Moses never wore the title "king," but he showed himself an ideal ruler. After a month-long trek through the desert, Moses was reunited with his father-in-law, Jethro, the Midianite. They shared experiences. Moses also kept up his rigorous schedule of judging. Jethro observed, however, that Moses was near exhaustion from his work of judging the people. Sub-judges, able and godly men from the nation (Ex. 18:13-27) and responsible for sharing court cases, could ease Moses' burden of governing.

Jethro suggested that a bank of qualified judges be set up to take the weight of judging off Moses' shoulders. Moses was in his eighties at the time. How did Moses receive Jethro's idea? He could have blown off steam and told Jethro to mind his own business. He could have taken offense at an outsider, a non-Jew, intruding into Hebrew governmental policy. But Moses did not resist Jethro's counsel.

One commentator thought Moses erred in listening to the Midianite. The truth is on the other side. Moses showed wisdom in not refusing the advice of a concerned relative. Octogenarian Moses did not react stridently, stubbornly, or scornfully. His response was neither hasty nor abrupt. Moses evaluated Jethro's suggestion and saw good in it. In being open to ideas from others, Moses showed himself the ideal senior.

BALANCED LEADERSHIP
MEANS SHARED ACTION

Power plays hurt profits in the business world. Delegated responsibility can be a step toward shared power. But it becomes bad bossing when one allows no feedback, no consultations, no openness to suggestions, no mid-course adjustments, or no acknowledgment of the contributions and talents of others.

Power struggles can degenerate into silly one-upmanship between cliques. Monopolizing is a sad denial of Christian maturity. Satan may not get us to fall flat on our faces before his own ambition for world control, but he gets his way whenever your or my goal is to "control" an organization—or, congregation.

It can be tempting to use our years as a hammer, beating on others. Yes, we've lived longer and seen a lot—including things that haven't worked years ago. But does that mean they can't work now in someone else's hands?

There are details in the Bible about older adults who had evil agendas and twisted morals. God included a few rotten elders in Scripture to remind us that while some of us mellow with years, others rage in age. Who are these wicked Bible seniors? Don't leave out the names of Eli, Jezebel, Maachah, and Athaliah. Others that could be mentioned are Saul in the Old Testament and Herod the Great in the New Testament. Every white head is not necessarily wise, kind, and godly.

Church bossism can take the form of fuming about emphasis on the Bible. I've found that any senior who can't bow head, heart, and knee to Christ's Word resists God's authority. Every so often one meets an occasional senior controlled by resistance to the Gospel. When Methodist bishop Frances Asbury [1745-1816] was thirty-four years old, a senior raised objections to his preaching of the Bible. Asbury described in his journal what happened after preaching on Acts 17:11 in Delaware (Oct. 11, 1779):

> ...I had a smart contest with a man upwards of seventy years of age, deaf to Scripture, sense, or reason, yet one that has been sorely afflicted; but age, like the word, if it does not soften, hardens.—*The Journal and Letters of Frances Asbury*, Vol.1:316.

Ironically, those who would be bossy are bossed. Part of being freed from the temptation to boss others is to recognize that bossy persons are secretly bossed—bossed by fears or old and hurtful memories, by abusive parents, by family history, by false guilt, by a drive to be perfect, and an inability to live with their own imperfections.

CONCLUSION

Bossism denies grace. Living by God's grace means that, in Christ, we are right with God while still sinners, while still imperfect. We continue to strive to become more like Jesus, yet there are things about us—and our spouses, and about our church—that probably won't get much better. No matter how much we pester, fume, and fret, those imperfections persist. What to do?

Live by grace with each other just as you live with Christ! Having fixed our eyes upon the miracle of God's grace, we understand each other through God's eyes.

God's grace chastens and corrects our leadership. Because by grace we are made captive to His power, we learn how to deal with others in our work, homes, and churches in patience. God is patient with us. We must be patient with each other. This big picture helps keep irritants and hurts from pushing others down. We learn mutual respect, the spirit of compassion, and the prospect that God uses all personality types for His own glory.

Howard E. Butt, Jr. was right in alleviating fears about adjustments:

> Health produces submission and submission produces leadership. Without this lesson we rule out human community. Submission steps down to lift authority up....Submission...never means your authority is wiped out: it only means your authority is willing to suffer...and grow.... Humility is not denying your gift. Humility is recognizing that your gift comes through you, not from you.[10]

WINNING WAYS

• Bossiness is a control game. It feeds our ego in an unchristlike way. God's rulership, not our dominance, however, is the Christian's goal.

• Not only "seize the day," but seize Christ to master your moods. We have not truly matured until we find where Christ's control begins and where ours ends.

• Sometimes we find it hard to give up involvement and we become intrusive. Retirement, in part, means we have surrendered some areas where we were once in charge. Growth is shown when we can relinquish our control to Christ.

• Manipulating others for selfish purposes pushes our agenda and is less concerned about achieving God's goals God's way. Prayer helps us admit to God's sovereign role and rule.

THINGS TO THINK ABOUT:

[1] Distinguish between boss and bossy, owning and possessing,—and possessiveness, interest, and obsession. Discuss how a Christian man or woman can be assertive without being bossy.

[2] How should Christians decide where we are stakeholders? Contrast how Moses and David dealt with shared responsibilities. As part of the church, what sets our limits of authority? Discuss the reaction of the man in his seventies Asbury mentioned and the acceptance of biblical authority described by Howard Butt, Jr.

[3] What psychological self-deceptions can be at work in the domineering personality?

[4] How can we allow space for others to be imperfect without abandoning our commitment to high standards?

[5] Manipulation for personal advantage goes on every day. What approach is more effective: the "soft sell" or the "hard sell"? How?

[6] Is pressing for greater effectiveness a form of bossiness?

[7] What role does Scripture play in establishing, guiding, and in challenging our authority?

4

TEMPTED TO BE INDIFFERENT

An old man going on a lone highway,
Came at the evening cold and gray
To a chasm vast and deep and wide.
The old man crossed in the twilight dim,
The sullen stream had no fear for him.
But he paused when safe on the other side,
And built a bridge to stem the tide.
"Old man," said fellow pilgrim near,
"You are wasting your strength building here,
Your journey will end with the closing day,
You never again shall pass this way,
You've crossed the chasm deep and wide,
Why build you this bridge at eventide?"
The builder lifted his old gray head,
"Good Friend, in the path I've come," he said,
"There followeth after me today
A youth whose feet must pass this way.
This chasm that's been as naught to me
To that fair headed youth may a pitfall be;
He, too, must cross in the twilight dim,
Good Friend, I'm building this bridge for him."
                    —Art Linkletter TV show: source

One job of the U.S. Bureau of Census is to project future age levels in our nation. By the year 2000, they expect that the percentage of teens in the population will be much lower than now. By 2025 there will be twice as many over age sixty-five than there are teens. Satan's biggest market is going to be seniors, whether he likes it or not. This population trend also should be a call to churches to get more serious and focused about senior ministries.

Satan may regard his work among seniors as a cinch. With them he may feel he has more elbow room, more opportunity to distract and to dupe. Temptations do not taper off with age. They do not de-escalate for older adults. When the years go *up*, temptations do not go *down*.

The Tempter's assault on retirees is not random, spasmodic, and token, but routine, repeated, and rigorous. Satan customizes temptations to our own circumstances, our weaknesses, our predispositions. He also is an expert at change of pace and surprises.

In Chapter Three we looked at the temptation to bossiness. Just because we aren't bossy doesn't mean we have given Satan the slip. He can get us with loss of will and with apathy. One of Satan's strategies is to lure us into indifference. Through our moods, tired muscles, and lazy habits, the devious prince of darkness gets us to drift apart from others, the church, and from God.

Don't assume Satan would rather fan the flames of youth than go after retirees. Isolation will not insulate us against temptation. Jesus was in the wilderness when He was tempted. We may be on edge of a wilderness, i.e., playing on a golf green, but Satan still comes after us.

Jesus may have had little clue about the siege of temptation that would beset him after his baptism. At that baptism, Christ's messianic role was announced.

There was a spirit of joy at the Jordan that day. But soon after his messianic mission was proclaimed, Jesus was put to the test. Satan entered the scene rubbing his hands, eager to get at Jesus. Right on the heels of so many fine spiritual experiences, we, too, may find Satan ready to pounce on us.

Most dangerous are those times when we are physically worn, weakened by sickness, sleeplessness, or sorrow. Satan romps in the favorite playgrounds of apathy and distraction. Another of his prime times is when a spiritual milestone is reached. We rejoice in it. We're...off guard, too. Jesus knew success in His baptism just prior to His wilderness retreat. Satan lurks in similar times for us.

CARELESS VS. CARING

Inattentiveness can become a form of indifference. Physical ailments, dementia, and senility can turn seniors who were once fastidious about their appearance into being oblivious of hygienic needs and cosmetic appearance. Poor nutrition, vitamin deficiency, poor circulation, and sleep deprivation can be clues to an apathetic state.

While short-term memory loss seems evident when repeated statements trigger no recollection, forgetfulness also can result from inattention. Inattentiveness can be a form of indifference. Indifference means we have given up our mental focus on a project, a cause, commitments, or goals.

Respect for the elderly is rewarded in Boy Scouts and Girl Scouts. Assisting seniors has always been one of the good deeds scouting has encouraged. Several years ago I saw a four-panel cartoon showing two boy scouts helping an elderly lady across the street. Things were going slowly. They seemed to have difficulty in getting her across. The scoutmaster happened to see it and afterwards commended them for their good turn. They replied, "It wasn't all that easy."

"Why?" asked the scoutmaster.

"She didn't want to go."

THREE TESTS OF GODLY CAREGIVING

"Caregiving" is now a popular phrase. More and more local churches are becoming very intentional about caregiving. Volunteerism seems to be growing across America. With cutbacks in governmental programs, volunteers are more essential than ever. Twenty-three million of our households are caring for ill parents. In our cities, there is a resurgence of both informal and organized neighborhood "watches."

But if so much of caregiving is good, does that make all of it godly? At worst, can caregiving become one of Satan's tools, an ungodly temptation?

Not only has Satan never abandoned his promotion of "me first" and "self care," but he also manages to work his way into altruistic and socially beneficial caregiving. After all, as Jesus' original encounter with Satan reminds us, Satan tempted Jesus in a holy place, for the desert was traditionally linked with holy moments in the life of Moses, John the Baptist, and others.[1]

Although in all three of Jesus' desert temptations Satan suggested that Jesus came first and that the needs of others were secondary,[2] we must not fail to realize that Satan can promote our self-justification through our deeds of mercy. To begin with, the patron of selfishness can make us proud we are caregivers. Again, caring in one area is thought to compensate for the lack of caring in another. Substitution of one act for another placates conscience and makes us see ourselves as caring individuals, so good that we think we don't need the righteousness of Christ. We can camouflage our avoidance of God's Word by our work for others.

Let's consider three tests for distinguishing *good* from *godly* caregiving.

First, is our caregiving done unto Christ or from lesser motives? In Matthew 25:35ff, our Lord not only commands caregiving by the righteous but identifies its highest level of motivation: "unto me." Now, of course this does not mean lesser motives are bad; they are just that: lesser. So what? As a general rule, the lower the level of motivation, the greater the risk of care failure when it's most difficult—especially with those we are tempted to judge as unworthy of it. Humanly speaking, it can be easy to care for those identified as "innocent." Not so long ago, for example, in divorce matters church people were accustomed to shunning the so-called "guilty party." But notice what Christ commands us in this Matthew 25 passage: "...you visited me in prison." Godly caregiving is to the ostensibly unworthy, but done unto Christ himself. That level of motivation overrides all-too-human temptations to withhold caregiving from those whom others might regard as "unworthy" of it.

A second test of godly caregiving is whether it happens no less in our own God-created personal relationships. Clergy may be especially tempted here, bestowing timely pastoral care on everybody while spouse and family get the leftovers—at best. Does our spouse/family get at least as high a quality of caregiving we extend to others? If not, our motives are more likely to be self-centered than centered in Christ.

Finally, is our caregiving founded on prayer and ongoing study of God's Word? It is a rare church that doesn't name—each Sunday—members who are sick, shut-in, or grieving. But how many of us take active *responsibility* for our prayers? And, how many work at equipping members to be able to articulate the healing

power of God's Word with those who need it most—
and where they need it?

Stand back from Jesus' three temptations. Notice
they centered on two appeals: (1) they tried to make
Jesus cave in to "self-care," and (2) they centered on
immediate gratification, to forsake his Alpha-Omega
name and nature.

When on the cross, Satan tempted Jesus to think of
Himself first. At both the Temple and on Calvary, Satan
made them places to show off—not places to *serve*. But
Jesus did not fall for the Deceiver's ploy either time.

INDIFFERENCE: AN OPPOSITE TEMPTATION

How can indifference have appeal? Wouldn't it be like
saying poison is healthy. How can indifference be a
temptation when indifference already has an evil reputation?

Four instances of indifference in Scripture should
warn us:
- indifference to Scripture (Hosea 8:12)
- indifference to Christ's death (Lam. 1:12)
- indifference to God's goodness (Job 21:13-15;
      Matt.22:15)
- indifference to suffering humanity (Luke 10:25-37).

Nonetheless, indifference can become an authentic temptation because it can become an easy way to escape
involvement. When we are afraid to set our hopes high
lest we experience greater disappointments, the pact
usually made with ourselves is: "don't wish for anything special." The absence of aspiration becomes attractive because one figures failure can't happen when
there are no goals to miss. Indifference lessens the risks
of exposing oneself to more pain.

A cynical detachment helps some of us to cope with

stress. "You can't be hurt if you don't feel," goes the reasoning. Apathy becomes a cozy wrap-around blanket insulating us against personal suffering. Holding oneself apart protects a person from loss if separation does happen. Not caring gets seen as a victimless way of safeguarding oneself from guilt, from worry, from embarrassments, and from over-stimulation. Apathy becomes the atrophy of compassion.

On the other hand, a callous, uncaring attitude toward another's woes is characteristic of the non-Christian, according to the Bible. "The righteous care about justice for the poor, but the wicked have no such concern" (Proverbs 29:7, NIV).

Can we afford such indifference? When it comes to being shoved to the back of society, most of us are unwilling to lay down and die. We will fight through AARP lobbyists, if nothing else.

In the days of the Old Testament prophets, senior concerns were not on the front burners of government. The plight of the elderly in pre-Social Security days often was ignored. Jeremiah lamented: "No respect is shown to the elders" (Lam. 5:12). It was an ancient instance of "ageism" (prejudice against the elderly). So the elderly would retreat from public ridicule (5:14).

Social *dis*interest has relational implications. The contemporary lack of concern for people's social needs is not primarily intellectual; it is spiritual....If a person has genuine encounter with God, his life will be transformed from self-seeking and self-aggrandizement to social concern, a concern for other people.[3] Social apathy is unbecoming professed Christians. It cannot claim support from the "God of all care."

The least lamented indifference, however, is indifference to the Word and presence of God. When God walked in the garden in the cool of the day, guilty Adam and Eve hid. When Christ came walking in the heat of the day, many people hid from the rays of His words behind masks of indifference. Unbelief includes the state of not caring what God has said, not caring what Christ has done. The gospel reflects God's care for sinful humanity, but the reaction in the world is non-caring disbelief.

> ...if our gospel is veiled, it is veiled to those who are perishing. The god of this age has blinded the minds of unbelievers, in that they cannot see the light of the gospel of the glory of Christ, who is the image of God. (2 Cor. 4:4, NIV)

Satan doesn't care for those he seduces into uncaring. He goes about as a roaring lion and has no remorse for the wasted moments, the wrecked bodies, and the wretched lives that result from tempting them into apathy and indifference—sins more common than blatant wickedness.

Christ's care stands in sharp contrast to Satan's strategy to deprive humans of spiritual emancipation. Formerly at a distance from God in our new life in Christ, we experience God's closeness and Christ's cleansing power. In this, by God's grace Jesus' care becomes visible and real through the likes of us.

> No one ever cared for me like Jesus,
> There's no other friend so kind as He;
> No one else could take the sin and darkness from me,
> O how much He cared for me.
> —C. F. Weigle[4]

In Christ we gain a new enthusiasm for God, for life, for others. God's Word alerts us to junctures where it can connect with—and heal—real needs, and it raises us to a new level of concern for others.

> [Against]...paralyzing apathy and the creeping recession of the will to live, the Christian faith must show

itself in courage for incarnation, in a passionate love of life, and in its ardent interest in existence, so that the feeble 'enjoyment' of life acquires the power to resist death, catastrophe, and all others who pursue them.[5]

If we are retired, we trim our budgets and keep them lean. But should we ever cut back investing in others? It is tempting to hurt less by hedging more. When we see a need, it's important to step forward to help as best we can. It is not Christian to spend life caring only for ourselves.

APATHY KILLS; AFFIRMATION REVIVES

In his latter years, England's famed social commentator, Malcolm Muggeridge, showed much enthusiasm for life. He found attitudinal inertia deplorable. He described apathy this way:

> ...just refusing to join in; lying inert in the bottom of the boat with the bilge water, indifferent as to where it's going and who holds the [rudder]...[6]

If bilge water in a boat's bottom is like apathy, by implication the water under the boat keeping it afloat symbolizes excitement. The analogy, however, also suggests a sadder prospect: that, for many, too much of that bilge water can actually steer—even sink—the boat!

Muggeridge was hardly alone in refusing to drift. In Cincinnati, where I live, I have come to know of John Henry Simmons of College Hill. As I write this, he is fifty-seven, a young senior. His life was turned around after he heard the Gospel in a testimony at his church by Bertha Carter, a civil rights leader from Drew, Mississippi. Prior to that time, Simmons led a life of crime. He had been charged with a variety of offenses: vagrancy, petty larceny, receiving stolen property, grand larceny, robbery, drug possession, and drug trafficking. Rather

than think his life was over and down the drain, he saw
he no longer had to be driven by evil forces.

John Henry Simmons is now a new man. He was
successfully treated at a drug facility in Kentucky. For
the last five years he has been creating new currents of
kindness where he lives. He founded a "Be Kind" movement. To promote kindness, he approached local busi-
nesses for their support to produce caps that carry two
simple words—"Be Kind." He has given away nearly
three thousand of them. As an acronym, "Be Kind"
stands for "Boosting Everyone's Knowledge, Integrity,
Nobility, and Dignity." In addition to giving away the
caps to everyone he meets, he "has embarked on a
campaign to bring formal recognition to people who
have done kind things and haven't sought notice for
them."[7]

When we shake apathy, we experience new health
and vitality. Psychotics and the suicidal know the crippling effects of apathy. Many who were suicidal tell
how they felt dead on the inside. For them life did not
simply slow down; it stopped.

Other consequences of not caring can be more trou-
bling because self-destructive hostility often accompanies apathy. Overcoming indifference is more urgent
than getting rid of crabgrass, coffee stains, tub rings,
and rust marks.

ZIP, ZEST, AND ZEAL IN CHRISTIAN SENIORS

"Zest" can refer to soap. "Zest" in the kitchen refers to
the yellow skin of a lemon that separates it from its inner
bitter white jacket; it is used to flavor salads, drinks,
deserts, and gourmet dishes.

Edward Gibbon [1737-1794] wrote a famous history
of the period in which Christianity began. In his massive
The Decline and Fall of the Roman Empire, he argued that

early Christian zeal was a carry-over from Judaism, not something generated from Christianity itself.[8] Narrow Jewish nationalism focused only on gaining Israel's independence. Was Christian zeal a carry-over from zealot nationalism? Hardly. The first Christians were on fire to missionize the known world for the apostolic Faith.[9] The enthusiasm that made them flaming torches of the Christian gospel came from an immediacy with Christ, commitment to His gospel, fanned by daily communion.

Christ and the Holy Spirit give Christians zest. He can flavor all we do and say. But that won't happen for those whose spirituality is distantly attached, disdainfully cool, or dryly interested. Spirituality doesn't become upbeat in a flash, but involves dedication to the struggle of shaping and sharpening our knowledge of God at the wellspring of truth, Scripture.

In a nursing home office, a secretary was asking an elderly applicant her answers to standard questions on her application for residency. Her answer to one section shocked the staff person. The admissions person asked her for her "zip." Without batting an eye, the older woman answered, "Normal for my age."

Christians know heart happiness. Rather than thinking senior celebrations unbecoming, abnormal, bizarre, or "not acting one's age," the prophet Jeremiah saw salvation as a joyful experience: "...young men and the old shall be merry..." (Jer. 31:13, NRSV).

Joyfulness is not something limited to youth. Retirement years can be effervescent. What makes a person happy despite the physical decline? Get reacquainted with the Lord in His Word, our greatest source of joy. Daily prayer and Scripture reading not only promote and prolong life, but they inject a spirited approach to problems and projects. Before God's throne of grace, gigantic problems become less threatening, big challenges become achievable, and major burdens shrink in significance.

Scripture rarely recommends retirement. Indeed, it implies that good health and skills make retirement an affront and irrelevant. In Exodus, for instance, there was no automatic cut-off age for retirement (35:22, 25, 26, 31-32). Skilled workers were encouraged to keep at their trade. Retirement came not at a certain age, but when one could no longer contribute.[10] Today, early retirement often leaves us with one-third of our life yet ahead. Should it not be spent in productive action, rather than dawdled away in nonstop leisure? Productive retirement can become a major motive for enthusiastic re-entry into a new work field.

Ezekiel refers to elderly men still working. Gebal, the seaport of Byblos, was a Phoenician coastal city where master shipbuilders plied their trade. It would be comparable to Bath, Maine, on the U. S. east coast, a port famous for modern shipbuilding. Unless ships were carefully caulked, they were not seaworthy and would surely sink. "Elders" in Ezekiel 27:9 were skilled ship caulkers, craftsmen expert in "coating with pitch" and "the doweling of the planks."[11] Their occupation was linked with Tyre's elder-nobles who also were not above doing difficult, exacting, necessary, but menial labor.

The underlying assumption in the Old Testament was that trades and skills should be utilized to benefit the nation. A role of the senior was to promote public good. That was held high. Skilled retirees also were encouraged to continue work and seek ways to prolong their employment. Though retired, our special talents can continue to benefit society. For some, this might involve delayed or deferred retirement.

One lesson from Ezekiel 27:9 is that modern elders should utilize their abilities as long as possible. Instead of avoiding new ventures, try one and excel at it! Lest we slide down to the isolate-and-vegetate lifestyle, seek out volunteer routes that not only help others but also keep us learning. In our recreational activities, be sure to include those that involve being with other people.

Too many seniors become indifferent to their usefulness. Our example can be like the veteran craftsmen of Gebal. Care! Improve, excel, enjoy, participate!

WINNING WAYS

• The temptation to say "phooey" when asked to try something new can disease our inner growth and vitality. Take at least one "people-risk" a week. Choose a new hobby—or a new skill with a hobby you already enjoy.

• An ability to fight off indifference is helped by spending time reading the Bible and praying—in ways we're not used to. There are some inspiring new translations. While reading them, new lights might shine from familiar jewel-like passages.

• When we soak up the sunshine of God's promises, our interests in God's style of spirituality increases and our love for others expand. In prayer, remind God—and yourself—of his specific promises.

• Spiritual productivity results from knowing and growing in Christ. Remember: God has never set an age limit on who can be useful for His glory!

THINGS TO THINK ABOUT

[1] What cares does God handle for us? What cares are we to handle for Him?

[2] Is anger *hidden* by indifference or does indifference result *from* anger? Cite some examples.

[3] How does a caring attitude promote and provoke positive action and response?

[4] What care projects are available to seniors in this area? Are there needs that have been overlooked? In the last year what projects have been undertaken? What new programs are being considered for the next year?

[5] The Good Samaritan cared. Why was that shocking? How did Jesus care for the Samaritans (Luke 10:25-37)? Did anyone else care about Samaritans?

[6] Should we care about those in despised classes and categories? How can the parable of the Good Samaritan apply to seniors?

5

TEMPTED TO BE
GULLIBLE

Satan's satisfaction is made complete when people are gullible to believe claims that he does not exist, or that he is neither interested nor involved in human history.

> Jesus met the reality of Satan and resisted. "Then Jesus was led by the Spirit into the desert to be tempted by the devil. After fasting forty days and forty nights, he was hungry."
>
> Matthew 4:1-2 (NIV)

Only someone mean would take candy from a baby, and only a manipulative crook would swindle a senior. Locally, *The Cincinnati Post* carried an article July 23, 1994 reporting the case of a senior swindled. read: "'Healer' Preyed on Aging, Ailing."[1] It told the story of a psychic healer who conned an eighty-three-year-old out of thousands of dollars.

We've all heard or read reports of local scams aimed at the elderly. These should remind all of us to use plain, old-fashioned common sense and be wary of strangers touting sensational bargains. Hesitating to believe everyone is not being overly suspicious; it is being prudently cautious.[2]

If hearing is failing, we can miss important points about a project or product. A business deal without a written contract or a craftsman without a verified work history and solid references should raise red flags for any of us at any age. Caution spares us trouble down the road. Suspicion can show shrewdness.

Older people continue to be exploited by uncertified contractors, by the "pigeon drop" scam, by door-ringers claiming to be from the utility or telephone companies, by mail fraud, even by their own greedy adult children. Be wary of "free offers," "lowest rates," and "opportunity-of-a-lifetime sales." Flimflam solicitors regard seniors as easy targets, aim carefully, and try to grab our retirement savings.

How can those unwilling to take such advice become gullible? "Old and set in our ways" would seem to be a sure safeguard against gullibility. Rigidity among many seniors would also seem to protect them from being "taken in." Simone de Beauvoir argued that old but great minds find it difficult to accept change and the new.[3]

One explanation for gullibility may be emotional starvation. In the face of a seller's charm, friendliness, interest, and signs of success, an emotionally-starved senior may relax his or her critical faculty, bend to pressure, and make an unwise decision. Special targets for con artists working an area are lonely retirees without a network of friends or nearby family to act as a buffer zone against unscrupulous scams.

FALLING FOR FOOD

Aging eventually gets us all. We know this but also need to realize there are ways to ease its toll. For example, when a hearing aid or new glasses are needed, we purchase them. At the same time, we acknowledge that aging can't be cured or reversed.

Sharp minds are enhanced by good nutrition. Though mineral and vitamin supplements are not "cures" for memory lapses, they help maintain our health and can prolong life. Calcium tablets (along with trace minerals) can help prevent ailments and slow or reverse some types of bone loss, for example. Eating wisely is crucial for good health.

Because of their modest prices, buffets are popular with many seniors. Someone speculated that old Methuselah would approve of frequenting "all-you-can-eat" restaurants.

> Methuselah ate what he found on his plate,
> And never as people do now,
> Did he note the amount of the calorie slate?
> No, he ate it because it was chow.
> He wasn't disturbed as at dinner he sat,
> Devouring a roast or a pie,
> To think it lacked unsaturated fat
> Or a couple of vitamins shy.
> He cheerfully chewed each species of food,
> Unmindful of troubles or fears
> Lest his health might be hurt
> By some fancy dessert:
> And he lived over 900 years.[4]

While some of us would be healthier if we operated on emptier stomachs, avoid becoming fanatical about dieting. By all means, do not starve yourself like a thirty-six-year-old man in Philadelphia who began as a raw food enthusiast, went further into organically grown food, and from there he approached total abstention. He wrote with pride in his journal of February, 1978 (a week before his death from complications of malnutrition!) that he was down to small amounts of sprouts, wheat germ, melon-rind juice, and raw fruits and vegetables.[5] He had made dietary discipline his religion. But it killed him.

Another direct link between diet and good health is the amount of plaque or blood "mud" in our arteries. Fish oil carries Eicosapentaenoic acid. It is the raw material from which the human body makes a chemical called prostacyclin. Prostacyclin—harder to say than to swallow—reduces cholesterol. Prostacyclin also helps stop blood platelets from piling up and forming blood clots. Medical consensus is that it protects the arteries against fat build-up, prevents clotting, and lengthens life. What we eat can lengthen life. Prostacyclin is a common by-product of eating fish.

Should I Swallow That?

Ideas are not untrustworthy because they are modern, nor are they condemned because they are old. Scripture reminds us that the old are not always right (Job 32:7-9; Ecclesiastes 4:13). Seniors and youths alike were exhorted to fair interchanges and a willingness to accept sound advice, not letting its proponent's age determine what is right (1 Peter 5:5b). One likely implication of Peter's counsel was that meekness in the elderly helps keep them forever young. Satchel Paige, the major league pitcher who was still playing at age forty-eight, said he knew "twenty-year-old guys with ninety-year-old minds and ninety-year-old guys with twenty-year-old minds."

The Gullible Fall for Phony Back-ups

Physical stress can produce bad choices. Our physical needs may create an openness to suggestions we would normally reject. A hungry person, for instance, is predisposed to believe someone's claim that food is at hand. Jesus' forty-day fast set Him up to be lured. Anyone who has gone without food for that long is interested in eating any bread, mildewed or stale.

Eating is fed by desire. That desire can inspire making bread as well as consuming it. In themselves, neither the desire to eat nor the desire to bake are evil. Satan, however, wanted to lure Jesus away from total dependence upon God and from completing preparation for His public ministry by using His normal need to eat.

Satan would urge us to think that divine wisdom can be gained through direct contact with God. But Jesus' citation of Deuteronomy was a reaffirmation of our need not to crave only direct conversation with God for guidance. Scripture supplies the best arguments and the best advice on what to believe and do. Our views on life, the world, and interpretations must be rooted in and regulated by the whole of God's written Word.

In Jesus' second temptation, Satan tried to get Him to seek back-ups, to get Jesus to rely on angels' catching ability. He asked Jesus to trust angels rather than just the divine promise of protection. Such overcompensation ploys are attractive to the gullible.

Modern Christian seniors do well to keep their eyes on God's previously given and proven faithfulness. Demanding angelic intervention shifts our focus from the Lord to manipulate His realm on our private behalf. By citing Scripture to rebut Satan (Matt. 4:7), our Lord was showing us how to evaluate a proposition or teaching—even when it seems to be supported by out-of-context citations from Scripture.

Satan took Psalm 91:11f (Matt. 4:6) out of context and tried to make it say what he wanted, but what the text never intended. "The psalm offers no encouragement to rush irresponsibly into peril or to seek an overt demonstration of God's promises."[6]

Jumping off a balcony or leaping from a moving train will not prove God's reliability. Such acts say more about one's sanity. Neither does impulsive risk-taking make the Word of promise surer. The so-called daring faith Satan asked Jesus to exercise was a ploy either to show that Jesus' comprehension was weak or that His faith was shallow. Jesus' response was that to test God was not to trust God, but to trivialize God's Word (Matt. 4:7).

Christians who practice poisonous snake handling on the basis of Mark 16:18, in effect, have fallen for the same tactic Satan used against Christ when asked to hurl himself from the Temple roof. A presumptive testing of God was never promised protection by God— either then, or now. God has not promised to nullify or reverse our dumb deed. Back-up assurances of God's truthfulness are not necessary.

CAN EMPHASIS ON "SIMPLE FAITH" PROMOTE GULLIBILITY?

Throughout Scripture, Satan's temptations were powerful because they presented single solutions simply. As far back as the Garden of Eden, Satan's appeal to Eve was a charmingly simple appeal to pride (or, in today's jargon, self-realization): "You shall surely not die....You shall be as gods, knowing good and evil" (Gen. 3:4-5). The power of a temptation can lie in its utter simplicity. Preservation, moral elevation, and spiritual self-determination were served up to the primal couple on the platter of simplicity.

Those who would belittle such distinctions should ask themselves what the simplicity policy would mean in other areas of life. Would we prefer a surgeon who makes quick incisions no matter where or why? Do we care when a pharmacist fills our prescriptions from any jar or bottle regardless of its content? On a cruise, do we want a captain who ignores charts, instrument readings, and weather reports?

[We] demand professionals thoroughly acquainted with the smallest details of their professions...We refuse,

therefore, to be influenced by the sickly talk about
simplicity regarding faith, or by the impious cry against
a so-called dogmatism, but shall diligently seek to give
an exposition of the being of faith, which, eradicating
error, will point out the only safe and reliable path.[7]

Christians, young and old, play into Satan's hands by
eulogizing simplicity to the point that they embrace
anemic teaching and shun continued growth in spiritual matters. Paul's desire to retain and recapture the
"simplicity that is in Christ" (2 Cor. 11:3) was not a call
to cut back on knowledge, nor an endorsement of vague
answers, nor a blast against learning. Rather the intent
of Paul was to adhere to clarity in the explanation of the
Gospel, to stay close to the core of Christ's teachings and
to a unity of purpose.

The context of the Corinthians passage where Paul
urges simplicity needs further comment. The quarrel-
ing Corinthians were disunited. Paul urged them to
wholeheartedly adhere to Christ's gospel. (The verb
[*aplothes*] translated "simplicity" also appears in James
1:5 where it is used of God: "God is a simple giver"—i.e.,
He is generous and straightforward.) The simplicity
Paul desired for the Corinthians had three components:
clarity of thought, single-minded devotion to Christ,
and unity of direction and discipline.[8]

Of course, Satan kept his approach with Christ simple.
Jesus' second desert temptation was an attempt to get
Jesus to limit His thinking to one text. Wrong conclusions usually result from insisting that one verse be
isolated from the whole living voice of God's Word.
Certain Jews tried this when they argued that Jesus
couldn't be the Messiah because everyone who died on
a tree was accursed—remember Absalom, for example?

The power of darkness would like to keep as much of
the Bible unused as possible, for therein lies the strength
of so much temptation. Taking a text in isolation often

shows that one does not see how it threads into the whole fabric of Scripture.

People become the prey for false teachings whenever they ignore context. Proverbs 14:15 (NIV) says, "A simple man believes anything, but a prudent man gives thought to his steps." To pit faith against reason and theology against life usually complicates trust rather than promote it. Moral fog generated by those lost in spiritual twilight repeat Satan's scam by insisting on simplicity to defend distorted ideas. Beware! Demands for simplicity may be a subterfuge to murder the gospel's living center and the Holy Spirit's action.

WAYS SENIORS CAN REBUFF SCAMS

[1] *Never make choices on the basis of appearances.*

It's easy to be fooled by wide smiles and warm embraces. Pay closer attention to matters of reliability, accuracy, and full disclosure. All eggs are not good; some are rotten. All mushrooms are not eatable; some are poisonous. All smiles are not genuine, for "one may smile, and smile, and be a villain." (*Hamlet*)

Technology has transformed complex principles of physics into useful tools. Caution, however, is always wise before heavy investment. Money brokers, bargain contractors, and health aid promotions ought to be scrutinized.

> As we grow older
> The world becomes stranger,
> The pattern more complicated..."
> —T. S. Eliot, *Four Quartets*

Even a sage needs a skilled interpreter. Consulting with reputable advisors with tested insights would spare us from shaky investments and unnecessary grief. "Inside information" or "getting in at the starting line" are favorite come-on scam phrases.

[2] *Prominence does not validate truthfulness.*

Piety and polish can become two more hooks Satan uses to separate people from their lives, savings, and destinies. Many families have agonized when an aging parent in a distant city has given substantially to televangelists whose track records have been marked more by greed than godliness. Countless innocent people have been "taken" by scams that tug on the heartstrings. Deceit is often difficult to uncover because the Master Deceiver has many agents—including those who use beguiling false sales pitches. Counsel still worth following:

> To be ready to accept any kind of message from a magnetic man is to lose the Gospel in mere impressionism. It is to sacrifice the moral in religion to the aesthetic. And it is fatal to the authority either of the pulpit or the Gospel. The church does not live by its preachers, but by its Word.[9]
>
> —P. T. Forsyth [1848-1921]

Fraudulent claims also creep into spiritual life scams. For example, does a pastor or church gouge, falsify, or divert church funds away from purposes designated by the donors? Some seniors are critical of teachings *outside* the church but so gullible about practices *inside* the church! Our critical faculties need to be exercised everywhere, because Satan is just as likely to try getting his way with us in the congenial atmosphere of a church as he would elsewhere.

Many Christians seem satisfied to judge a program, an organization, or theological idea the way they select an airline: for convenience, comfort, and economy. A bird may have the head movements and profile of a woodpecker but not the inclination, ability, or determination to punch holes in trees. So also faith touters may have the right dress, decorum, and dossiers, but only when their teachings are examined carefully are departures from biblical norms uncovered. One reason why there is lack of both biblical conformity and Christ-centricity goes back to superficial knowledge. For example, over one-third of the senior pastors of today's mega-churches do *not* even have a seminary degree! Calvin cautioned "...exercise discrimination, and [do] not suppose as a matter of course, that all who call themselves pastors are so in reality"[10]

[3] *Sound judgment is not made on a feeling level.*

Euphoric or good feelings about something or other may be the only proof some seek. "It just feels so good." Satan, however, uses *romanticism* as much as *reductionism* to increase his net gains. Ernest Hemingway, the novelist who committed suicide, put morality on the basis of feelings with his famous line "good is what you feel good after and bad is what you feel bad after." Unfortunately, even Abraham Lincoln naively accepted as true the statement of a man named Glenn whom he heard say in church, "When I do good I feel good; when I do bad, I feel bad; and that's my religion."

What is morally right and what is true theologically should not be judged by the psychological "kick" it delivers. It is dangerous to measure truth with an emotional thermometer.

Feel-good Christianity eventually produces anti-Christianity. "The emphasis upon the believer's feelings," warned Britisher Alan P. F. Sell, "has not only encouraged anti-intellectualism [against learning, JG] in some varieties of conservatism, it has also spawned antinomianism [do-as-you-please, JG] in ethics."[11]

"To limit religion to feelings does not maintain its independence, but undermines its existence."[12]

For feelings come and feelings go,
And feelings are deceiving;
My warrant is the word of God,
Naught else is worth believing.
Though all my heart should feel condemned
For want of some sweet token,
There is One greater than my heart,
Whose word cannot be broken.
I'll trust in God's unchanging word
'Till soul and body sever;
For, though all things shall pass away,
His word shall stand forever.

—Martin Luther

[4] *Keep Christ as the final standard of truth.*

The Christ of Scripture is our authority. When the salvific importance of Christ is dismissed, minimized, or reduced, we set ourselves up for the Deceiver. Former FBI head, William Webster, tried to improve the Federal Bureau of Investigation by "de-Hooverizing" the Bureau. Christianity is not improved but impoverished by two trends: to *de-Christ* salvation and to *de-Scripture* Christ.

The Christ of Scripture should be our test instrument. Raymond Brown translated 1 John 4:3b: "...everyone who negates the importance of Jesus reflects the spirit which does not belong to God."[13]

A critical mind, rooted in Scripture, focused on Christ and rounded by a grasp of Christian experience and precedents throughout history, will go a long way to expose shoddy scholarship, sly manipulation of the biblical text, and so-called special spiritual insights promised by slick promoters.

Care in discernment, wrote the apostle John, should characterize all Christians regardless of age. He wrote—

Dear friends, do not believe every spirit, but test the spirits to see whether they are from God, because many

false prophets have gone out into the world. (1 John 4:1,
NIV)

Charles Haddon Spurgeon [1834-1892] told of what
happened to Robert Hall [1764-1832], a brilliant student
who graduated with a M.A. from Aberdeen University.
He began with liberal theological tendencies. Eloquent
and popular, Hall eventually served Saint Andrew's
Street Baptist church at Cambridge.

He returned to restudying and even reproaching
many current Protestant teachings. He referred to this
period of his ministry as his "conversion." Several Cambridge church members found his preaching increasingly irritating. Some were annoyed enough to object to
his preaching of salvation through the Cross of Christ.

Several dissatisfied members met him in the vestry
and said, "Mr. Hall, this will never do."

"Why not?" he asked.

"Why your sermon was only fit for old women."

"Why is that?" he probed.

"Because they are in need of comfort, tottering (as
they are) on the borders of the grave."

"Well, then," Hall said, "you have paid me a high
compliment, for if it is good for old women on the
borders of the grave, it must be good for you, if you are
in your right senses, for on the borders of the grave are
where we all stand."

WINNING WAYS

• Swallowing pills is usually a snap. The regularity of taking them once or three times a day may make us psychologically open to accepting other things. Beware: gulping down a sales pitch can be dangerous to our financial health and well being.

• False beliefs are often hard to detect when wrapped in skillful and seemingly sincere presentations. As we should ask questions about our medications, so we should ask questions about truth claims.

• A wise Christian senior should hesitate to latch onto slick ideas and promotions. The Devil's favorite form is that of an angel of light.

• Review the Four Tips in this chapter on how to detect imposters.

THINGS TO THINK ABOUT:

[1] What is gullibility? Is Christian faith itself gullible?

[2] Why is apostolic Christianity less likely to encourage gullibility? Were the apostles gullible about our Lord's resurrection?

[3] Give some examples of gullibility in your own experience or among those you know. For instance, how does initial sales resistance turn into mistaken acceptance? How have usually skeptical and suspicious seniors been "taken"?

[4] Review the attempts of Satan in the two major temptation stories (Genesis 3 and Matthew 4) to get the primal couple and then Christ Jesus to fall for his scams. Note any parallels (other than terrain and climate) and significant differences.

[5] What ways can retirees use to protect themselves against smooth talk that lacks reliability and substance?

6

TEMPTED TO
LIVE IN THE PAST

Only by looking back at the wake on the ocean can one
see the direction that the captain is guiding the ship. So
it is in life. When we look back and see how God has
been present in our lives, we are assured that he has no
intention of leaving or forsaking us.[1]
                                    —Win Arn with Charles Arn

Though occasionally misused and subject to lapses,
memory should not be maligned. There is a richness to
memory that supplies us with insight and inspiration to
help us deal with a sometimes grizzly present and
unknown future. Memory is an ever expanding library.
Especially happy are those who recall biblical texts and
truths. King David valued memory. Once his safety
depended on and was due to the memory of others. For
example, there was the memory of Shobi, the Ammonite
(2 Sam. 17:24-29; 19:31-40).

HAPPY SPIRITUAL MEMORIES

Ours is the God who "remembers," sometimes in judgment, more often in blessing. The Bible is the supreme
remembrance book. It is the record of God's events

recalled by participants and eyewitnesses. Scripture also exhorts us to use our memory of God's acts and their meaning for us.

Again, David set us an example. "I dwell upon the years long past, upon the memory of all that Thou hast done." (Ps. 143:5, NEB)

Old Testament believers found refreshment in recalling God's goodness in the past. Reminiscing is recommended to inspire us about past achievements and successes. A personalized review of what has transpired can lift our spirit in an atmosphere of worship. Consider Psalm 42:1, 2, 4 (NIV):

> As the deer pants for streams of water, so my soul pants for you, O God. My soul thirsts for God, for the living God....These things I remember as I pour out my soul: how I used to go with the multitude leading the procession to the house of God, with shouts of joy and thanksgiving among the festive throng.

In the New Testament martyred leaders were worth remembering:

> Remember your [deceased] leaders, the men who spoke the Word of God to you; look back upon the close of their career, and copy their faith. (Heb. 13:7, Moffatt)

Biblical nostalgia gets a bloody nose in some circles. Appeal to the past for standards is looked down upon as rigid and irrelevant. But memory of what once happened is divinely sanctioned and spiritually sane.

Memory can be as much God's tool as Satan's. G. C. Berkouwer reminds us that historic reformation landmarks were a boon for solving problems in the later church. Our theological predecessors viewed the original Protestants with profound regard. They had "a passionate, critical concern for the present and the future of the church."[2]

One generation praises God's grace to the next generation. Pastor and hymn writer, Augustus Montague Toplady [1740-1778] admired and commended the message of fellow Anglican evangelist George Whitefield [1714-1770]. In turn, Whitefield used and commended the relatively recent writings of John Bunyan [1628-1688]. And Bunyan had benefited from Martin Luther's [1483-1546] commentary on Galatians. Without mining gems from a useful past, present gains may be shallow and short lived. Life is too brief to reinvent it from scratch. Memories that do not ignore our predecessors' experience and mistakes pay us well in the future.

CAN THE PAST BECOME SATAN'S WEAPON?

Nostalgia can choke progress, however, when it becomes a cheap escape mechanism. How we remember our past determines whether it immobilizes or improves us, whether it motivates us or caters to stagnation.

Going back to something called "old time religion" can become a disguised form of burying one's head in the sand. Face it: our message is apostolic, not just old! Our sentiments need to go past our grandparents to Christ's grand first disciples.

Get a fix on the past's good without letting it become a crippling fixation. What hurts is thinking that faxes from the past are enough for the present. To ignore present questions means we have lost touch with life. Cherish the good in the past, but don't ignore the present. It's bad to let past memories make one indifferent to matters needing attention *now*. The problem is not the past, but in becoming its prisoners, in letting it blind us to the potential of "at hand" opportunities.

We best cope with our circumstances when we focus on the present in light of the past and future. That becomes practical Alpha-and-Omega living. The key is lordship—who's in control of how the past works in our lives. If our use of past hurts, gripes, and grievances are self-centered, our past becomes Satan's deadliest weapon against Christians. One of its common forms? When we say: "I'll forgive you, but I'll never let you forget it!"

Try to live by hope as well as by memory. The difference between anxiety and hope about the future is a question of control over the future: do we try to control it, or does Christ? The same question decides when the past is the kingdom of guilt for us, or the realm of assurance and blessing.

Counsel from Biblical Seniors

Consider these biblical downsides of nostalgia from the lives of Abraham, Reuben, and Job. Abram took a nostalgic trip back to the sacred spot where he first worshipped Jehovah (Gen. 13:3). He had been in Egypt and his faith had faltered (Gen. 12:9-20). He discovered that Egypt was as corrupt as the land he had left. Being somewhat anxious about Sarah not bearing a child and feeling down from having been in Egypt, he returned to the place of his prior dedication to God (Gen. 12:1-7). His nostalgic trip had a bitter outcome. Strife developed in his own clan (Gen. 13:7,8). Abram was delivered from jealousy and greed, but he didn't want discord and disunity to occur in his family.

Reuben was eaten up by bitter nostalgia (Gen. 42:22). Regrets can be like a ravenous fox hidden under our coats. In time they will chew at us. Nostalgia can become neurotic.

> Remorse, the fatal egg by Pleasure laid
> In every bosom where her nest is made.
> Chagrin can hatch into catastrophe.
>   —John Milton

Ancient Job seems to have dallied with what modern psychology calls "infantile regression." Job was robbed of energy by excessive preoccupation with what once was. His five-fold sighs about "when" showed emotional collapse, a kind of swoon (Job 29:4-25). He said, "If I could only go back to the old days, to the time when God was watching over me, when his lamp shone above my head" (29:2, NEB).

Where we experience God is less important than *that* we have experienced him. Moses was delivered from an unhealthy nostalgia. After Sinai he never called the people to return to Sinai for worship. With the exception of Elijah, there is no Old Testament record of Sinai as a pilgrimage site.[3]

Samuel admired the past acts of King Saul. This admiration had a powerful influence on Samuel, making it difficult for him to realize God had removed His hand of blessing from Saul.

> The Lord said to Samuel, "How long will you mourn for Saul, since I have rejected him as king over Israel? Fill your horn with oil and be on your way...."
>
> (1 Samuel 16:1, NIV)

Samuel was called to look ahead. But his nostalgia became a sterile stare to the rear. Saul was still the official king, but Samuel held onto the hope that Saul's position would remain secure. But, in so many words, God said to Samuel, "Break with the past and look forward. Get ready for another anointing."

Isaiah, the prophet, jolted his audience from being hung up on the sandbar of memory:

> Forget the former things; do not dwell on the past. See, I am doing a new thing! Now it springs up; do you not perceive it? (Isaiah 43:18, 19, NIV)

On the Mount of Transfiguration Peter would have been content to contemplate endlessly those two wit-

nesses from the past and Christ's triumphal glory. But
Christ wanted his disciples to come down from there
and gear themselves for a new future. That time of
prayer and praise was meant to prepare them for the
next adventure, additional pages of new history.

The author of Hebrews warned against "shrinking
back" (3:12). Paul F. Schmidt saw in this phrase a reference to psychological regression:

> Negative growth back towards infancy is the response
> called 'shrinking back' by the author of the biblical
> letter to the Hebrews.[4]

> "A cake made of memories will do for a bite now and
> then, but it makes poor daily bread."
> —Charles Haddon Spurgeon [1834-1892]

Paul Tournier, the Swiss psychiatrist, went further: "I
am not one of those who sigh for the good old days,
which were not good at all, and which would be intoler-
able today."[5]

THE PAST IS TEMPTING

Satan is a wizard with nostalgia. He brought up old
verses to get Jesus' respect, attention, and compliance.
Satan used the best of Israel's past to tempt Jesus in the
desert. Two themes were prominent in the second temptation: One was to invoke the Temple; the second was to
misuse verses from Psalm 91. Satan put these two together and suggested that Jesus throw himself down
from the peak of the Temple, citing the Psalm's promise
that the angels would "act as a net" to catch him in his
fall (Ps. 91:11,12).

Satan not only believed in God; he read and used the
Bible. It was as though the Devil carried around his own
"pocket copy" of the Psalms. Did Satan see a connection

between the Temple's architecture and God likening Himself to a mother eagle that cushioned her eaglets against their fall? (Ps. 91:4; Ex. 19:4 repeated in Deut. 32:11) Psalm 91, Satan suggested, ideally applied to a high point of the restored Temple. But Psalm 91:4's phrase about being borne on eagles' wings seemed to match one architectural feature. Austin Farrer noted that the gable end of a roof was known as an "eagle," for it projected outward and forward, "so the side cornices or eaves became the wing-tips."[6] Marvin Vincent suggested that "pinnacle" should have the sense of "wing."[7] Divine mercy is the "catch all" for falling fledglings. Perhaps.

Just as intriguing is the possibility that Satan was out to show his contempt for the angels he had left as well as for the Lord. Satan was more into thinking of "falling" than "catching," given his own biography. The idea of falling came naturally to Satan. He went through a great fall much more serious than what happened to ill-fated Humpty Dumpty. Satan rebelled against God and fell from heaven. Did he subconsciously wish for Jesus to mimic the agony of his own fall? Or did he just want Jesus to smash Himself into oblivion? There can be little doubt that Satan felt contempt for the angels who stayed loyal to the Lord. By misusing this Psalm passage for a false mission, Satan showed his undying contempt for God's angels as well as for Jesus.

Satan conformed far closer to Temple *architecture* than he did to the *meaning* of Psalm 91. Satan abused the past promise. He left out 11b—"in all thy ways"— which removed "the vivid idea of walking on a hard stony path"[8] The Psalm's promise did not include the notion of walking a narrow ledge, a thin line, or a tight rope, of being suspended high above the ground. The promise had nothing to do with being protected from a long fall under a bright sun at high noon, but with stubbing one's toe on a journey. The place where protection had been promised was not on a dizzy height, but on a dangerous path. Satan was twisting the Psalm's promise.

Another abuse of this promise was to suggest God put it there to "tempt" believers or to dare God not to fulfill His word. The promise of angelic intervention had nothing to do with those who would jeopardize their lives by thrill-seeking events that might go awry, for example. God has never promised a spectacular rescue for those who foolishly fling their bodies into a deep pit or catapult over a porch rail. The promise was for those engaged in routine matters, who go about their regular work and try to conform to God's will as they do so. The point of the promise is His protection of believers in ordinary affairs. There is no suggestion that our protection would be assured in presumptive and deliberately dangerous acts.

Satan targeted Jesus' physical condition. He could not disorient Jesus. But he could try to take advantage of Jesus' exhaustion. The temptation about leaping from the Temple was a mental trip. The only mental jump in the passage was from the desert to the city, not from the height of the Temple to the ground below. What is left unsaid in the passage was [1] how the Devil took Jesus to the Holy City, and [2] the specific spot from which Jesus was to jump.

The transferal to the Holy City was not an astral "trip," an out-of-the-body leap, for there is no suggestion that Jesus had left the wilderness. There, Jesus was in the last stages of a prolonged fast, a condition favorable to waking visions.[9] This temptation could have taken the form of a vision or a form of hallucination—but not the kind that loses touch with reality and God's truth. Prolonged hunger can contribute to dream states just as Joseph experienced earlier in the Gospel of Matthew.

Certainly, if Satan tried to take advantage of Jesus because of His famished condition, Satan also will try to take advantage of us when our bodies are worn down or worn out. Our inclination to doubt God, to take dares, to say and do rash things can increase with diminishing physical strength. Therefore, it is essential for Christian retirees to retain strong mental health, to absorb and have greater commitment to biblical direction. When tempted by unwise risks put forth in the name of faith, we shall then be able to refute and repel those suggestions.

What Happens When Memory Fails?

A memory failure can spare us pain when memories disturb. Some bad experiences can't be forgotten completely. Daily reminders can rile us. Tattooed prisoner numbers from Nazi concentration camps can bring back painful memories. A quadriplegic, whose life was tragically altered by an auto, skiing, swimming, or trampoline accident, illustrates how trauma jangles our memories. The past can pound us from fathoms beneath.

Sometimes a person in an accident can't remember it. That is called retrograde amnesia. Retrograde amnesia is one way our bodies react to horrendous abuse. When those assaulted or injured cannot recall details of the incident, they can become temporarily unconscious. Retrograde amnesia is our body's instinctive defense mechanism that spares recollection of pain. Amnesia avoids stress by loss of memory.

Most people, however, experience forgetfulness in smaller doses. We know it as "selective memory" where we forget the unpleasant but remember only the good. Memory can serve as an unexpected and merciful safety zone. Forgetfulness can be a blessing in disguise. Memory loss can spare our sanity and allow us to function without being haunted and hounded by the past.

Unresolved conflicts rarely are forgotten, however. Our psyche, unwilling to forgive, shoves resentment below the surface. Whatever is below surface consciousness can dominate from that position. Indeed, from there new spiritual poisons can originate. Unforgiven attitudes are ready-made channels for new grievances; they carry forward new attacks and new forms of bitterness.

Intense, deep, and lasting anger at God agitates rather than silences memory. Anger at God can render inoperative both retrograde amnesia and selective good memories. Isaiah's imagery about the wicked person's mind-set explains how subconscious resentments become conscious complaints.

> But the wicked are like the tossing sea, which cannot rest, whose waves cast up mire and mud. "There is no peace," says my God, "for the wicked." (Isaiah 57:20 NIV)

One of the bloodiest battles U.S. Marines fought in the Pacific theater of World War II was on Iwo Jima, a sliver of land five miles long. For thirty-six days after the Marines landed on February 19, 1945, Japanese and American forces battled fiercely. There were 6,821 American and over 22,000 Japanese defenders who died in that conflict. Three decades after the battle, waters around Iwo Jima still churn up buried debris from the clash. The remnants of battle—boots, helmets, stray weapons—are cast up by the waves.

Our subconscious is like an ocean bottom. Strange and sinister objects lurk down there, waiting for a raging storm above to call them up. The wicked are like the sea around Iwo Jima. The carnage from interpersonal battles, buried long ago, often reappear from the briny deep. Emotional jetsam surfaces from Davey Jones' locker of unresolved anger. Scrap metal pieces from earlier wrecked relationships surface. From one's churning subconscious come forth unresolved hatreds, buried hurts, and forgotten grudges.

Christian faith relies on the hospitable union of memory and hope, and both prepare us for the future. Hope replaces anxiety, and that hope encourages us to interpret and accept the future.

For Christians, what rules our future is what Christ did for us in his life, death, resurrection, and ascension. Nothing we have done for Him compares to what He has done for us. His past, more than ours, determines where we are and shall be. Our center of gravity, the place where we find balance and stability, is Christ. Unless our pasts are handed over to His Lordship, we can have no meaningful life in the present and no confident future.

Why would we want to dwell in the "good old days" when a new Eden lies ahead of us? Christ triumphed in history. He is the secret to the eternity ahead of us.

> [The Christian] expects to be happy one day, and this expectation causes him to pass over the happiness of the present. He is never, in memory and hope, wholly himself and wholly in his present. Always he either limps behind it or hastens ahead of it.
>
> The work of memory on life's past is bound up with the work of hope on its future. The meaning which we see in our future determines the significance we ascribe to the past....We...remember past experiences, not under any compulsion to repeat them, but in freedom, so as to be certain of our destination.[10]

The past can be powerful, so powerful that it keeps tens of thousands of psychiatrists in business. But Scripture supplies what no therapist can. It calls us to the past of Christ and how that supremely helps us in all ages.

Never are we closer to the benefits of Christ's accomplishments, victories and successes than right now. God surrounds and supports us in His love and grace, preventing Satan from finally jeopardizing our enjoyment of life in Christ. Christ defeated the Accuser—he who would use the past against us— on the cross and by His resurrection. We can enter the newness of God's grace in Christ confident in his lordship over our past with its mine fields, the present with its pain, and the storms that may lurk ahead.

In summary, retirees have five reasons why we can overcome a hurtful past:
— Why let the past victimize us when Jesus Christ is Lord of how the past and future work in our lives?
—Why live in our *own* past when there is greater healing from *Christ's* past?
— Why live in a past we cannot change? Let go of the past, and hand its hurtful power over to Christ.
— Why let our past poison our present and future?
— Why limit the operations of God's grace to former times? Grace works no less powerfully today!

When you resort to remembrance of the past,
— make sure the focus is God's goodness and grace;
— seek forgiveness and reconciliation from God for your responsibility in fractured relationships;
— let good memories renew your hope for God's future blessings;
— in recalling blunders, be sure to notice the happy outcomes;
— when past sins cause pain, remind yourself that in God's memory they are not only forgiven but forgotten—their power to hurt has been bound to their moment of forgiveness (Leviticus 16; Matthew 18:18).

WINNING WAYS

• Satan wants us to drown in our past. Begin by focusing on God's involvement in your life today.

• Avoid thoughts of "the good old days" to take over your outlook, or the Devil may succeed in making us spectators on the sideline of life. Center on the present's opportunities and potential. Participate!

• Our purpose in living is to make our present history more Christ-centered, more God-confident, not to keep banging our heads on past matters that can't be changed.

• Rivers are dredged of silt to make safe passage for large boats. Dragging to the surface old hurts, only to let them sink again, insures that our spiritual journey will be stuck over old wrecks.

• Be on guard: When God casts our past sins (and hurts) "into the depths of the sea," Satan will keep inviting us with "let's go fishing!"

Things to Think About:

[1] What are your earliest memories? What are your first memories which had to do with Jesus, Christians, the church?

[2] Have details about hurts from the past been dressed up to be a frequent guest or to discern God's blessing in their outcome? Sometimes we stop at exposing our true feelings and fail to experience God's forgiveness of what happened. Write down—in a Dear Lord letter— things from your past which trouble you. Then, seal the letter in an envelope. Pray: "Lord Jesus, I hand these matters over to you." Finally, burn the letter as a burnt offering to the Lord.

[3] What is there in a Christian's past that can better prepare us for the present and future? Could it be that God's time differs from ours? How does Scripture view God's time? Is time ruled out of eternity? (See Chapter 8 of my book *Probing Heaven,* where the relationship of time and eternity is discussed at some length.)

[4] When early Christians referred to conversion as a "second birth," did they want to be stuck there? Or were there other purposes for a mature Christian life?

[5] How does Christ's past relate to our own past experience with Him?

[6] In what ways does Christ's lordship over how time works—how it participates in our life—direct, control, and shape our past, our present, and our future?

[7] Discuss meanings—for everyday living— of the text: "Jesus Christ, the same Yesterday, Today, and Forever." (Hebrews 13:8)

7

TEMPTED TO FANTASIZE

...how few in the world...[are]...made better by age. Generally, they will see, that such leave not their vice, but their vice leaves them, or rather retreats from their practices, and retires into their fancy; and that, we know, is boundless and infinite: and when vice has once settled itself there, it finds a vaster and wider compass to act in than ever it had before.[1]

—Robert South

The sight of a shimmering water pool ahead on a road through a desert is an illusion. The French word for it is "mirage."

Whereas "mirage" is an external visual trick, "fantasy" is internal. Mirages are physical. Fantasies are mental. Imagining is done inside our heads. Fantasy is "advanced imagining"—something we invent inside us.[2]

Jesus was tempted to fantasize abundance of food, miraculous safety, and global domination. When Jesus neared dehydration in the desert's arid atmosphere, Satan held out to Him the prospect of fresh bread and a cushioned landing. If Jesus had jumped off the Temple's high point, it would have been the ego trip of all time, bringing him an oasis of ovations from nations in exchange for servitude to Satan.

We can identify with Jesus' temptations when our surroundings are Spartan, far different than sizzling sand. When circumstances become difficult, we can be tempted to let our minds wander to better times. We imagine successful windfalls that could quiet feelings of failure. Some fantasize luxury rather than meager circumstances. We dream of plenty to compensate for want. Or we fantasize about renewed virility to compensate for nearing impotence.

WHERE DO OUR FANTASIES GO?

Reverie (reflection on the past) is not necessarily fantasy, but it can head in that direction. Fantasy focuses on the past or future in order to ease pain from former times or dread of the future. Our past can charm as readily as make us cringe. Recollections can become disguised future dreams. Innocent reverie verges on temptation when it creates a reality divorced from fact.

Fantasy uses fertile imagination. Everyone has the capacity to imagine, but not everyone uses it to escape from a failed past through increasingly grandiose daydreams. Imagination also is a basis for role playing. When we role play, we visualize an action, event, or object. Role playing can facilitate empathetic entrance into another's perspective and situation.

Imagination is active in our dreams. In a sleep-state, dreams are acted out. Dreams can both use action and compensate for lack of action. We dream of being, doing, or experiencing our worst fears or our best hopes. But why limit imagination's exercise to sleep? We also can let our imaginations run free in our conscious moments. "A man without imagination is more of an invalid than one who lacks a leg."[3]

The Tempter likes to lasso our imaginations. But where imagination rules out rational oversight, evil can grow. Inclinations can shift toward intentions. Intentions can slouch behind our imagination. An early biblical reference to this pattern is found in Genesis 6:5 (NIV), a text that described pre-flood humanity:

> The Lord saw how great man's wickedness on the earth had become, and that every inclination of the thoughts of his heart was only evil all the time.

Christian parents can be troubled by fantasies pumped and pushed at their children by the entertainment industry. During the month of December, some Christian parents tell their children that Santa Claus is fiction. Ironically, many of these same parents allow their children to dress up like witches and monsters on Halloween.

Other Christian parents permit the Santa fantasy but tell their children that there is a difference between fantasy and reality, that some people replace Jesus Christ with Santa Claus. Some wisely note that Santa Claus was a godly pastor who gave people gifts at Christmas time. Such caution and corrections are at once consistent with the centrality of Christ yet show compassion for children's love of fantasy. "Make believe" is fun for children, but fun must not be an excuse to neglect developing their critical faculties.

When we reach our senior years, are we free of fantasies? Is our capacity to dream as strong as our inclination to nap? Scripture refers to ungodly dreams (Gen. 6:5) and to godly dreams. Acts 2:17 (cites Joel 2:28-32) is an instance: "....your old men will dream dreams." Capabilities for fantasy continue into our senior years.

Some hymns promote fantasy, prodding our spiritual imagination. The spiritual, "Were you there, when they crucified my Lord?" is an example. We see ourselves "there" where Christ was crucified for us. We are better able to grasp the gravity of God's placing the guilt of our sins upon Christ at Calvary. Elizabeth C. Clephane [1830-1869] described our experience:

> Upon that cross of Jesus
> Mine eye at times can see
> The very dying form of one,
> Who suffered there for me.

Fantasies free our minds from pressure and enable us to distance ourselves from sufferings can with positive effect. But,

> ...there is always the risk of [dreams] becoming too detached from reality, being nothing but an escape, a pure fiction. And in old age, it may be nothing more than an excuse.[4]

Where do fantasies come from? They bubble up from experiences, from frustrations, and from anticipations. Godly dreams come from God. Ungodly dreams come from our evil nature and Satan. The well is deep on this matter, but adult fantasies can be disguised rationalizations. When unresolved guilt, crushing failure, and low self-esteem refuse to die, to fantasize is not a realistic solution. Dangerous fantasies, the ones that become temptations to sin, are those that encourage us to ignore, devalue, and distort reality. Evil fantasies create false realities.

Satan inspires the fantasy that we always win while others lose, for example. This borders on illusions of grandeur. We must be critical of immodest hopes that build on other people's troubles. Innocent reverie takes on the profile of temptation when it becomes a reality-denying fantasy. As well, falsely imagined threats have one foot on perverse fact-land and the other on paranoid fantasia.

Our memories can be healed by God's grace, but not unless remembered wrongs are handed over to Christ. Showing Jesus our painful past—specifically naming its features—is the first step toward healing its hurt. "If we confess our real sins, God is faithful and just and will forgive our sins." (I John 1:9) Healing love becomes a reality when Jesus is invited to become the ruling Lord of our broken past.[5]

SATAN USED FANTASY AGAINST CHRIST

Satan works through our minds as well as our human drives. Recall that Satan's temptations of Jesus primarily addressed His mind. For us, as well, temptations to evil are going to be turned back at the mental level.

Seasoned elders pride themselves on long-lasting mental commitments. Although hormonal output diminishes with age, our minds still teem with a surplus of ideas. Thoughts are powerful in revising the present and in shaping the future. One's mental drive is often the last physical power to go.

Jesus' first temptation in the desert (making bread from stones) was primarily mental, not gastronomical, because Satan appealed to our Lord's awareness of His ability to make bread. Satan's temptations aimed at Jesus' capacity for fantasy along with His power to establish reality. Forty days and forty nights of fasting could make fantasy come easily. Jesus suffered dehydration, and we know dehydration can induce dream-states.[6]

Fantasy was a major factor in Jesus' desert temptations. Angels coming to His aid was never something Jesus could only dream about. Angels were always available to Him, even in the desert (Mark 1:13). While the third temptation encouraged fantasies of grandeur, the second temptation was primarily concerned about self-preservation and pumping up someone's ego.

The third temptation was about immediate world acceptance. Its purpose was to divert Christ from his road to redemptive death. Likewise, seniors may fantasize honor and recognition without suffering. If Jesus would only acknowledge Satan's bogus rights, Jesus was offered no more hunger pangs, no injury from leaping, and no opponents to overcome. Similarly, Satan would seduce us into thinking that we can get rich and gain renown without effort, without hard choices, and without patient endurance.

FANTASIES FOR SKEPTICS

Many still consider a supernatural God as fantasy. Satan gets people to believe there is no basis in reality for belief in God. Freud, Feuerbach, and Marx believed that God was an unsubstantiated thought, a projection from craving safety in a menacing world. Arnold Toynbee believed that God was merely a "feeling" welling up from a deeper level of the human psyche. Even belief in Satan many consider a fiction. Too few regard Satan as a real personal being. Sociologists may refer to belief in Satan as an instance of "reification" in which an abstract idea is presented as a concrete reality. But the Bible's point about Satan is this: Evil is not a concept but an extremely *personal* experience.

Historically, Christianity emphasizes a material reality. Against the egocentric Gnostic spiritualizers of the first century, Christ's tangibility took on central importance. Unlike unbelieving scoffers, the early church "apparently knew how to distinguish between ecstatic visionary experiences and fundamental encounters with the resurrected Lord."[7]

Arguments that the early disciples were prone to visions is rightfully undermined by the fact that they didn't expect to see a risen Christ. Indeed, they were reluctant to believe in Him. Yet the confirming appearances were not a few isolated cases, but many. Repeated simultaneous—and so similar—hallucinations by different groups at different times were extremely unlikely. When evaluated by advanced modern historiography (vs. outmoded nineteenth-century "historical positivism"), Christ's appearances have all the qualifications for historical events rather than imaginary occurrences.

> I love to tell the story.
> More wonderful it seems
> Than all the golden fancies
> Of all the golden dreams....
> —Catherine Hankey [1834-1911]

Our future expectations, drawn from the Bible, have credibility because of the supernatural, yet historical person of Christ. "Without the transformation immanent in the system the future transcendence of the system would become a powerless dream."[8]

Non-Christians vary in beliefs, but they usually hold in common a belief that the individual is the final authority. Inherent self-centeredness neither commits to responsibility for others nor to the authority of a divinely-inspired Bible ends with self-approved fabrications ("vain fancies" [Ps. 73:7, NEB]) as one's guideposts.

How eager were Jesus' critics to compliment themselves about how they would have acted differently than their predecessors when God addressed their own failures.

> You build tombs for the prophets...you say, 'If we had lived in the days of our forefathers, we would not have taken part with them in shedding the blood of the prophets.' (Matt. 23:30, NIV)

Theirs was a case of adult fantasies about the past. The

point Jesus made was that they would have not acted any differently than their forefathers, for in the rejection of Christ, they showed the same spirit as in the rejection of the martyred prophets.

SENIOR FANTASIES EVOLVE

Early childhood fantasies enable abused children to survive trauma. If a child is excessively threatened by the success of other children, he or she is likely to hide rage and envy by fantasizing his own successes. While under the umbrella of his parents' reputation, a child may spin himself a protective cocoon of grandiose self-importance.

When seniors feel trapped, they may use fantasy to escape. Fantasy can blunt and absorb inner pain. Instead of a bruised ego resorting to alcohol, hypochondria, or unfulfillable daydreaming, fantasy helps to ease the pressure. Remorseful introspection, on the other hand, unknowingly conceals a rebellious self-destructiveness.

We may carry fantasies from middle years into retirement. Retirement is a time to reformulate and revise them. The past may be refreshed, but the future is still open, which may be why fantasies on the past can have greater attraction. "The aged man's inward experience of his past takes the form of images, fantasies and emotional attitudes."[9]

New fantasizing features emerge in retirement. The lily is gilded in daydreaming; trumpets and flourishes are added. Former hopes are revised and reshaped to provide new support. A retired worker may flatter himself by embroidering small past successes far beyond what originally happened. Favorable embellishments are added to enlarge his sense of worth.

Many retirees scoff at attempts to reconstruct the

past. They aspire to happiness, acceptance, and a sense of youthfulness, not through skillful revision but through daring experimentation—and even exchange. For instance, how many older folks have thought their situation would improve if they had a much younger spouse?

Proverbs 12:11 (NIV) warned: "He who chases fantasies lacks judgment." Christian seniors need a governor not only over their mouths, but on their imaginations, because fantasies can become self-defeating and destructive if they are allowed to control our actions...and decisions. Egotism and power hunger often dominate and motivate dreams. Ambitions, apprehensions, and unfulfilled desires float to the surface in our fantasies.

We can't bring our thoughts to Christ's ownership without subjecting our wishes, dreams, and projections to the scrutiny of Scripture. Christian psychologist Wayne Oates warns:

> ...Fantasy that is sealed off from reality is thereby cut off from the ethical perceptions of the person and may break forth in irrational actions. Thus testing of a fantasy against reality never happens. [10]

Scoping Coping

Too much time spent dwelling on the past subjects us to a needless emotional drag. It increases our fears and guilt. Dream regressions in senior adults become infantile wishes projected on the future. One way we cut free from fantasy domination is—realistically—to accept and work on our past and its defects. We also keep in mind that the past will continue to grip us unless we seize the present and become Christian stewards of our tomorrows.

For the insane, dream and reality are one. Unable to cope with the real world, the psychotic retreats into his fantasy world. Paranoia is a mental condition in which threatening impulses are projected on the world around us. Mental illness intrudes upon many rapists, satisfying their aggression and repaying some surrogate victim for a supposed sexual humiliation sometime in the rapist's past.

Sometimes fantasy can protect our mental health. POWs have been spared mental collapse by using their imagination to escape their horrible circumstance. When in a Nazi death camp, the late psychiatrist Victor Frankl [1902-1997] reminded himself that the reality he was in was far worse than his fantasies of freedom.[11]

Children's fantasies are epitomized in the epic fairy tales of J. R. R. Tolkien. He wrote a massive 1,200-page trilogy about Middle-earth and the activities of elves, dragons, trolls, men, wizards. Of course, hero Frodo Baggins and his fellow "hobbits" are also therapeutic and entertaining.

When we reach our senior years, we can have nightly dreams that permit us to go safely "insane." We may seek to resolve problems through dream pictures. Thus, our dreams turn into disguised fulfillments of frustrated wishes. What we can't resolve in our conscious life we answer in our waking dreams.

RETIREE FANTASIES

Retiree fantasy often is about appearance and attractiveness. One leading adult fantasy is immunity to decline. Perhaps you have seen the T-shirt slogan "If things get better with age, I'm approaching Magnificence!" An opposite fantasy sees only doom. A son of Korah foresaw his premature death. Psalm 88:15 (NIV) reflected: "From my youth I have been afflicted and close to death." It reminds me of the eighteenth-century Christian journals of Cotton Mather and Frances Asbury. Both men seemed sure that their current ailments would be their last.

Seniors need to be on their toes (if not on their feet) when it comes to speculation on their longevity. Our energy level can be lowered by constantly looking back. Excessive dwelling on the past distracts and depletes. Obsession with the good old days can make us resentful, regretful, and remorseful. Some dreams should be dismissed; others are to be transcended.

Fantasy also plays a significant part in mistrust. "Delusion" is a favorite biblical equivalent for fantasy. Delusions are fantasies that work against us, although they might first emerge as helps. The Bible refers to delusions of various shades and intensities (Ps. 4:2; Isa. 44:20; Jer. 14:14; 23:26; 2 Thess. 2:11; 2 Pet. 3:6; Rev. 19:20). Have you had doubts about a friend's motives or intentions? Have you entertained the possibility that you may be projecting your fear, dislikes, self-mistrust, and self-hate?

Psychiatrist Paul Tournier shared the case of a woman who always had trouble interpreting/reading railway schedules because her father had made her feel incapable of doing so as a child.[12] When a son has hostile feelings against his mother, living or deceased, these feelings can be transferred to his wife. And disdain for his wife may be transferred to "her" children.

"Old age inspires apprehension," wrote Christopher Lasch,[13] and some apprehensions are transformed into fantasies. Augustus Hopkins Strong [1836-1921], an American Baptist theologian, saw a grim future for himself when he was sixty-one years old. His major work, *Systematic Theology*, was in final revision (or so he thought). He wrote, "...I am as vigorous in my teaching as ever, but I well know that my strength must soon decline [yet he was to live twenty-four more years!] and work must become more and more of a burden."[14] Strong was not strong enough. He anticipated a sharp decline in productivity. He falsely predicted loss of creative energy. Yet God allowed him to expand his major work three times, the last one when he was eighty-one years old. (Strong's mistake was similar to Isaac's miscalculation of how much longer he would live. Isaac lived forty-three years after he blessed Jacob.)

In his autobiography Strong recalled a story that rebuked his own presumption.

> When I attended the party given to Mrs. Abelard Reynolds on her hundredth birthday, I asked one of the ladies present if she would choose to live so long, provided the choice were left to her. She hesitated a moment and then said: 'I would prefer to have someone else choose for me.' [That gave Dr. Strong pause to ponder; he drew back from his earlier dreary forecast.] And so I prefer that God should choose whether my life is to end soon or late, for I know that 'all things work together for good to them that love God' [citing Rom. 8:28]. [15]

Fantasizing about the future is futile. Plan wisely for the future. But forget about what is dimly ahead and do what is clearly at hand. Many of us are not overworked so much as over-worried.

EROTIC FANTASIES

The "vile abomination" of Ezekiel 8:9 may have been erotic fantasies. What the eyes could not see, the mind projected (Ezek. 8:12). Some hold that the "filthy dreamers" of Jude 8 were individuals consumed with erotic dreams. [16] W. Somerset Maugham [1874-1965] alluded to his own erotic fantasies when he wrote in his autobiography:

> How many of us could face having our reveries automatically registered and set before us? We should be overcome with shame. We should cry that we could not

really be as mean, as wicked, as petty, as selfish, as obscene, as snobbish, as vain, as sentimental, as that...[17]

Senior men sometimes fantasize sexual prowess because they fear castration. Erotic deliria are products of their own self-doubt, deteriorating sexual potency, and even feelings of aggression against the opposite sex.[18] Obsession with erotic thoughts at any age also can be an attempt to avoid thoughts of one's own death. Such activity arises from a hidden, intense anxiety and relieves accompanying tension. Researchers believe compulsive erotic thoughts compensate for male impotence or its impending onset and to convince mates that they are not dying or near death.

BIBLICAL REALISM

Why spend energy and time on dreams? The biggest boost is not to what our individual fortunes will be. What sustains us as we grow older is God's grace and sovereignty, Christ's victory, and the witness of the Holy Spirit to our reconciliation and life in Christ.

Christ's life, death, burial, resurrection, and ascension are not religious fiction. Our minds return again and again to solid biblical facts. The value of Jesus' life did not arise from the empty dreams of a few disciples. Rather it is the foundation upon which the entire Christian enterprise builds. Whatever seismic personal anxieties may shake us can't topple the fact that Christ died for us and that our eternal life was Christ's purpose and mission. We are fortified in hope, joy, and peace from the strong currents of Christ's life, death, and resurrection.

WINNING WAYS

• An active imagination is a spark God can use to have us discover new ways of serving Him. Avoid letting your imagination degenerate into a morbid preoccupation with obstacles.

• So many of our dreams are not worth remembering with their bizarre twists and mixes of no practical value. Avoid making too much out of dreams with little practical value.

• Goal setting is a form of conscious dreaming. Set your sights on accomplishing specific goals that can bring satisfaction to you, happiness to others, and glory to God.

• What occupies the living Christ is not pipe dreams but realistic goals, which only He as God can bring into being. The real Jesus has created spiritual realities for us and others that can never vanish and fade as human fantasies do. Count on it!

THINGS TO THINK ABOUT:

[1] What is a fantasy? How does a Walt Disney fantasy differ from private fantasy? Can recollection, reverie, and remembrance be part of fantasy? What percentage of past experience in a fantasy makes it more history than fantasy?

[2] Is all fantasy fiction? Isn't science fiction fantasy? Ancient mythology was storybook fantasy, exploits projected from real life onto imaginary people. Although not discussed in this chapter, what are several definitions of "myths"? Relate them to fantasy.

[3] When is fantasy beneficial? When does it become unhealthy? Fantasy can relate to the past, the present, and the future. Give one example from each time period.

[4] Does the Bible prohibit the use of fantasy when it insists on always telling the truth (e.g. Ex. 20:16)? Does this mean children should be denied hearing animal and cultural fables, e.g. Aesop's, Santa Claus? Elaborate on godly dreams (Acts 2:17). How are godly dreams checked and channeled?

[5] Can fantasies be used by Satan to derail our Christian commitment? What is a healthy relationship of Christians to fantasy and reality? Is prayer just a wish-projection, a fantasy given over to God?

[6] Should retiree fantasies be given a *carte blanche*? How can retirees be encouraged to dwell on their dreams or give greater attention to realities and God's promises?

∼ NOTES ∼

8

TEMPTED TO COMPLAIN

A little seed lay in the ground and soon began to sprout,
'Now, which of all the flowers around,' it mused, 'shall
I come out?'
I don't want to be a sunflower,
for the sunflower is too tall and ungainly, and has no
grace or charm.
Neither do I want to become a rose,
for the rose is rather loud in color,
has thorny stems,
wilts quickly, and isn't at all practical.
I certainly don't want to be a violet,
for the violet is too small, too uncolorful,
grows too near the ground in such secluded spots.
And so it criticized each flower, this supercilious seed,
until it woke one summer hour and found itself a weed!
—Author Unknown[1]

Admittedly, computer memory can be faster and more reliable than human memory—except when the computer is "down" or doesn't have enough memory. We should always find it more fun to tap a senior on the shoulder for a recollection than to press keys or move a mouse. Does "old" go with "good"? Do you agree with these pro-senior adages:

old wood is best to burn
old books are best to read
old friends are best to trust
old wine is best to drink.

Yet the Bible's emphasis is not "good and old" but good when older. Sooner or later we need what's "new." If our licenses expire, we're grounded. Not everything old will do. Old criticisms are like dull and rusted saws. Old complaints give "old" a bad name. Nothing makes newness old as fast as complaining.

God has heard endless human complaints. Few were good enough to get into the Bible. The Book of Psalms preserves fourteen "complaint Psalms." Nine are personal complaint psalms; five are corporate complaints.[2] Many who journeyed with Moses were not "happy campers," for they grumbled in their tents (Ps. 106:25). But complaints are not only in Scripture; they saturate the air around us.

A thirty-year-old novitiate in a Trappist monastery kept the "house rule" of uttering only one complete sentence every ten years. After his first ten years, the monk was invited to speak a sentence to the monastery Superior. It was this: "The bed is too hard." Another ten years passed. His second chance to speak to the Superior came. He said, "My room is too small." Another ten years passed. Again, when his turn came to speak, he uttered another short sentence: "The food is lousy." The Superior leaned back in his office chair reflecting. Then he commented: "Brother, you've been here thirty years, and all you've done is complain."

Ever hear a person growl without showing his teeth? Who are the complainers? Teenagers can whine like a rusty movie reel. When the garbage cans are overflowing and the grass nears knee high, how many parents have heard "there's nothing to do." Or another favorite teenage complaint: "there's nothing to eat." Yet refrigerator compartments and kitchen cabinets are well-stocked—but with despised nutritious foods.

Is Complaining Legitimate?

What does complaining accomplish? Is it a temptation to evil or a rite of passage? Some can't enjoy life without ventilating objections. Chronic grumblers are fussy, nit-picking caricatures of Scrooge's "Bah. Humbug." On the other hand, what you may regard as complaints, I may see as valid criticism.

When we get older, we expect better service, better products, and better treatment. What is "better," of course, often boils down to individual preference. If a product is of poor quality, if craftsmanship is shoddy, complaints are in order. How else is a company to know that its design or service is defective? Mediocrity can't be corrected unless it is identified.

From a family's point of view, one of the most hurtful complaints is when elders "openly complain how their children care for them and try to get others to take their side against the very people who are knocking themselves out on their behalf."[3] Next are complaints about poor health. "How can complaining be sinful when I'm just honestly recognizing changes in my body?" Those suffering pain should consult health-care personnel. Perhaps the distressing condition could be eased or eliminated. People need to express their legitimate complaints in a calm and frank manner, eliminating shabby attitudes or snapdragon dispositions.

Jean Jacques Rousseau [1712-1778] lamented at age sixty-five that his creative energy had faded. "Already my imagination is less vivid, and it no longer glows as once it did at the view of an object that stirs it into life.... A lukewarm weariness drains my faculties of all their strength; little by little the spirit of life is going out...."[4]

Sir Winston Churchill [1874-1965] led a charmed life. Yet in his later years he complained, "it is hard to find new interests at the end of one's life." J. Ernest Breed, M.D. was of the opinion that "a patient's complaint about his arthritis is merely a ruse for him to obtain sympathy and understanding."[5] Body complaints can become attention-getting devices. Attention no longer required by work is transferred to our bodies. We may complain of aches and pains to hide from ourselves the fact that we are suffering from a loss of standing.[6] Some retired seniors seem to become professionally sick, making the rounds of physicians.

Moses may have had a touch of that. In his great Psalm on aging (Psalm 90:9) he said "we finish our years with a moan." The NEB and REB read: "our years die away like a murmur." The NASB has "we finish our years like a sigh." The New Berkley Version broadens the figure to include the days leading up to the last: "...we spend our years as a sighing." "Moan with" [Ps. 90:9] is a Hebrew compound emphasizing life's weariness. The same word is used in Job 37:2. There the image is rumbling thunder. The usage in Ps. 90:9 from the Hebrew root *hagah* means to murmur, to mutter, to growl.[7]

Sometimes life ends with a series of sighs. Unattended sighs can graduate into grating grumbles. Constant complaints tend to wear everyone out and, in some instances, may make one's condition worse.

SCORCHED-EARTH COMPLAINING

Grumbling is a spin-off from the compare-swear cycle. Glorifying the past makes the present look inferior and keeps us in the dumps. How do we react to present events? Are we upbeat and positive, or negative and difficult to please? Do others hear us dwell on petty irritations? Do we sound like a trapped devil rather than a thankful saint? How we react is up to us.

> Some murmur when their sky is clear,
> And wholly bright to view,
> If one small speck of dark appear
> In their great heaven of blue.
> And some with thankful love are filled,
> If but one streak of light,
> One ray of God's good mercy, gild
> The darkness of their night.[8]

WHAT'S EATING YOU?

Suppose an honorary appointment or an award has been announced and someone far less qualified is given preference. Do we eat our hearts out because we were passed over? Do we gnash our teeth and say we should have had the honor? The Devil would like that. So why not give it to the devil, seeing it is his kind of dish? At this time in our lives how foolish it all seems! God is our inheritance and reward.[9]

We can improve our environment by being thankful. Whereas *grousing* make us and others miserable, *gratitude* clears the air and refreshes all of us. Rather than indulging in "wish-I-had" or "wish-I-was" notions, we would profit better by focusing on our gains, God's generosity and gifts, and on their distinctive worth and value.

> If you can't be a pine on top of the hill,
> Be a shrub in the valley, but be
> The best little shrub at the side of the rill:
> Be a bush, if you can't be a tree.
>
> If you can't be a bush, be a bit of the grass,
> Some highway happier to make;
> If you can't be a muskie, then just be a bass,
> But the liveliest bass in the lake.

We can't all be captains, some have to be crew,
There's something for all of us here;
There's big work to do and lesser to do.
And the task we must do is the near.
If you can't be a highway, then just be a trail;

If you can't be a sun, be a star,
It isn't by size that you win or you fail—
Be the best of whatever you are.
—Author Unknown[10]

Looking for God's goodness in all circumstances and valuing life's gains keeps us in a healthy mental frame. Sherwood Wirt's testimony challenges us.

I refuse to waste any of these wonderful days on this marvelous planet grousing, complaining, mulling over disappointments, or expressing any disgust over things in general....I have retired from all that. I prefer to look for the best and keep my hopes high, and right now I'm looking for a reason to celebrate.[11]

WORDLESS COMPLAINTS

William Cowper [1731-1800], neighbor of John Newton, chided sour Christians who were fluent whiners. In the second section of *The Olney Hymnal* (Hymn #60), Cowper wrote:

Have you no words? Ah! think again,
Words flow apace when you complain,
And fill your fellow-creature's ear
With the sad tale of all your care.
Were half the breath thus vainly spent,
To heav'n in supplication sent,
Your cheerful song would oft'ner be,
'Hear what the Lord has done for me.'[12]

Since nobody wants to be shunned as a complainer, complaints may be internalized. We clam up rather than clobber someone. Complaints can come across through silence...a look...a stare...a glare. Withdrawal of approval is complaining on another level. It is a wordless complaint, the "silent treatment." Pulling back or holding back are silent complaints. Blame-casting diminishes others. Disdain is kept out of sight, yet it causes minor mistakes to be blown out of proportion.

In the parable of the Prodigal Son, the complaining elder brother may have represented the complaining Pharisees (Luke 15:1,2). The elder brother showed himself to be an articulate complainer (Luke 15:25-32). One part of his gripe was that what he accused his father of not having done the same for him as he had done for his younger brother (15:29), which was a sign of deep jealousy. The other part was to suggest that the father's lavish welcome was unearned (by his wayward brother) and overdone (15:30).

Jealousy fuels the person who puts others down. Those criticized may begin to believe the complainers, when, actually, it is their talents and successes, their admirable qualities that ignite the criticism. A complainer argues that "so-and-so" doesn't deserve awards, advancements, contracts, and compliments. Acute envy denies others recognition that the complainers secretly cherish and crave for themselves.

SATAN, THE ARCH COMPLAINER

Jesus endured forty days of self-imposed abstinence. There were no "watering holes" to ease His distress. Our Lord's mind was not occupied with satisfying His appetite but with providing a solution for Judaism's spiritual aridity. Through His steadfast prayer, Jesus showed determination, dedication, and discipline.

Jesus was so unlike Moses at the same age. But like Moses in his later years, Jesus felt the pressure of time. Forty days without food made time drag. And plenty of time made the absence of food more tormenting. Jesus experienced one phase of aging without being old: He felt isolated. But Jesus did not complain.

Satan is not only the biggest liar, he is the all-time worst grudge-holder and grumbler. Satan complains although he enjoys the luxury of not being hungry. Undoubtedly, Satan muttered under his breath his never-ending blasphemies against God for his original banishment, even at the tempted Jesus. Satan acted like Israel did against Moses. Ironically, Israel's complaints to Moses were similar to Satan's temptations of Christ. Structurally and tonally, what Israel shouted at Moses Satan whispered to Jesus (cf. Ex. 17:7; Matt. 4:9).

For both Moses and Jesus, at issue was the validity of their spiritual leadership. Israel questioned Moses' ability to lead, and Satan challenged Jesus' ability to rule. In Christ's temptations Satan acted like a gargantuan Israel. Satan mimicked Israel. But now the stakes were cosmic.

On eleven different occasions Israel complained, from before and throughout the Exodus.[13] (For the specific passages, Israel's grumbling score card, see endnote.) It was not the number, however, but intensity of Satan's complaints against Jesus that stand out. Jesus did a much better job in putting the Devil in his place than Moses did in keeping Israel at bay and in line. Moses' pointed answers did not put to an end a complaining Israel.

Paradoxically, the murmurs of leading Jews against Moses were an anachronistic precursor of Satan's complaints against Christ in the desert. Christ is greater than Moses because He is the very source of divine truth. He is greater than Moses in that while He also received voluminous and virulent complaints directed against God, He *is* God.

Christ's life and ministry recalls much of what Moses endured. Jewish gripes against Christ compared to the

Jews' murmuring against Moses with one exception: Whereas the Israelites in the desert stopped short of murdering Moses, key Jewish leaders of Jesus' day would not be deflected from getting Christ executed.

"Murmuring"—the wilderness word—occurs once in Matthew (20:11), once in Luke (5:30), and four times in John (6:41, 43, 61; 7:32). Its usage in John's Gospel especially develops and draws out the parallels between Moses and Jesus having to endure human unbelief (cf. John 6:41-43; Ex. 15:24; Num. 14:2).

The imperfect tense of "murmuring" in John 6:41-43—i.e. "kept murmuring"— means it was unrelenting. "Complaining" in the New Testament includes a variety of synonyms. Whispering (*diagoggozo*), mentioned in Luke 5:30; 15:2; 19:7, was of the negative sort similar to the muttering of the wicked (Pss. 37:12; 38:12; 106:25). Although Mark did not characterize the statements of the disciples (6:35, 36) as grumbling, what they said was tantamount to complaining that Jesus detained them too long.

The sense of formal complaint (*entugchano*, root) was used by Luke to describe a petition of the Jews against Paul before Agrippa (Acts 25:24) and by Paul of Elijah's complaint prayer about Israel's killing of the prophets (Rom. 11:2). A formal petition occurs in Rom. 8:26,34 and Heb. 7:25.

"Groaning"(*stenazo*) in James 5:9 referred to inner despairing or sighing, rather than outward complaint (cf. its positive use in Mark 7:34). Objecting against the Word of God was a mark of apostasy (Ps. 106:24-26; John 6:41, 61, 66; 8:47; Jude 16 [*goggustes*—grumblers; *mempsimoiros*—complaining]).

SENIOR COMPLAINTS

Different complaints occur in what some call the three major stages of senior years:

the young elderly (age 65 to 74)
the middle old (age 75-84)
the ancients (85 to past 100).

Each stage has its own problems, adjustments, pressures, and needs. Complaints vary according to what
one faces. Fewer complaints seem to come from those
with tolerable good health. We are more likely to be
distressed by the loss or impairment of a faculty at a
younger age, when one expects to be vigorous and
active than during later years. As seniors, we expect
many of our capabilities to slow down. For example,
failing eyesight bothered Isaac (Gen. 27:1), Jacob (Gen.
48:10), and Eli (1 Sam. 3:2). Not much was made of that
loss, possibly because this ailment was widespread
among the elderly in those days.

Scripture promotes the ideal of life without complaint. Paul wrote, "Do everything without complaining or arguing, so that you may become blameless and
pure, children of God without fault in a crooked and
depraved generation…." (Phil. 2:14, 15b, NIV).

An acronym has arisen in adult ministries. Seniors
are (affectionately?) referred to as "grumpies" (grown-
up mature people). Better to be a among good-natured
"grumpies" than join the chorus of those who sing the
anonymously composed "Grumbler's Song":

In country, town or city, some people can be found
Who spend their lives in grumbling at everything around;
O yes, they always grumble, no matter what we say,
For these are chronic grumblers and they grumble night and
        day.
They grumble in the city, they grumble on the farm,
They grumble at their neighbors, they think it is no harm;
They grumble at their husbands, they grumble at their wives,
They grumble at their children, but the grumbler never thrives.
They grumble when its raining, they grumble when it's dry
And if the crops are failing, they grumble when they're high.

They grumble all the year round and they grumble till they
>   die.

CHORUS:
>   O they grumble on Monday, Tuesday, Wednesday,
>   Grumble on Thursday too.
>   Grumble on Friday, Saturday, Sunday,
>   Grumble the whole week through.
>   —Author Unknown[14]

CURBING COMPLAINT

[1] *Some complaints are valid and beneficial—*

Relationships improve when we learn how to phrase
comments positively. A legitimate criticism may carry
some sting, but when put constructively it is not received as an attack. Suggestion: Frankly examine the
motives behind our own critical remarks. Distinguish
between indisputable facts and subjective reactions,
between their presentation and our perception. Don't
unload all reactions at once. Share observations incre-
mentally. A dumped bucketful of complaints will only
run off, but a suggestion is more likely to soak in when
presented by itself. Avoid sarcasm, caricatures, and
speculation about another's motives.

[2] *Understand what fuels complaints—*

Collected injustices are the ammunition of machine-
gun murmurs. Differences not discussed, hurts not re-
solved, and grudges that are not let go spark and supply
our furnace of inner fury. Excessive and unrelenting
complaining, psychologists point out, arises from anger
over one's own faults, disappointments, and guilt. Murmuring against others usually arises from hidden self-
hate. Antagonism gets projected onto others rather than
directed at one's own faults.

People often spout sour attitudes because they crave
recognition and respect. We are tempted to chop away

at others' ladders to fit our own shorter reach. But a busy person is less likely to turn into a crabapple. Indolence and isolation are not healthy for seniors. By not participating in programs and projects, we can feel neglected and vent our frustrations. But when, for example, we share in our local church's workload, everyone benefits.

[3] *Learn to laugh—*

The late George Burns (born Nathan Birnbaum) was, bar none, the oldest stand-up comic. At age 98, he entertained at Cincinnati's Music Hall (May 1, 1994). He began, "It's nice to be here. At 98, it's nice to be anywhere." (A standard Burns opening line.) For 35 years he fed straight lines to his purposefully daffy wife, Gracie Allen. "By the time I found out I had no talent, I was too big of a star."

From Burns, we can learn to bounce back from sorrows. Gracie's death (August, 1964) was a severe blow to George's happiness, but he went on with life, performing on stage and writing. His only movie before Gracie's death was *In Honolulu* (1939). In 1976 he earned an Oscar for best supporting actor in the film *Sunshine Boys.* He also was a hit in the *Oh, God!* films. Burns' longevity and our longevity are mostly the result of God's goodness and partly of our ability to laugh. Burns said, "When I walk out on the stage, I really forget my age. The audience makes me forget. The audience gives me vitality."[15]

[4] *Acute Complaining Backfires—*

Expressed grievances often don't produce positive results. Indeed, the reverse often happens. Movement stops; openness shuts down. Why? Complaints can be taken as an attack on one's person. No one likes to be thought of as being wrong, and no one really wants somebody else highlighting his or her faults. Regretfully, what is complained about often materializes.[16]

[5] *Complaining is sin—*

Israel's murmuring against Moses was ultimately directed at God (Num. 14:27). People who complain that God is silent in their times of turmoil and tragedy want God to intervene immediately—and on their own terms. To them God seems either too slow or too remote, so they keep trying to write their own life's script. That same person may complain about God when he picks apart people's well-intended, but imperfect service.

[6] *Grumbling is unChristlike—*

Jesus' statement that "foxes have holes and birds have nests" (Lk. 9:58) was not a complaint, but a response to the superficial would-be disciple who professed that he would follow Christ anywhere. Jesus threw out a challenge; he was not griping. Up to the cross He nobly and bravely absorbed a mounting series of injustices and insults from a succession of antagonists. Peter wrote that it is better for us to let offenses pass and refrain from tongue-lashing than to attempt to retaliate or rectify our reputation by pulling others down (1 Peter 3:9-14). The old spiritual described Jesus' demeanor through His trials:

> They crucified my Lord,
> And He never said a mumbalin' word!
> Not a word, not a word, not a word.
> They pierced Him in the side,
> And He never said a mumbalin' word!
> Not a word, not a word, not a word.
> He bowed His head and died,
> And He never said a mumbalin' word!
> Not a word, not a word, not a word.

[7] *Contentment with God reduces complaints—*

Instead of bewailing the fact that we can't have all we want, we should be thankful we don't get from God what we think we deserve. We don't "deserve" eternal life, do we? Indeed, have we deserved any of life's greatest blessings He has given us? So, whenever we feel the temptation to complain coming on, stop to count our blessings and name them one by one!

[8] *Squelching criticisms will not stop them—*

Several years ago now-retired printer Richard S. Frederick of Mechanicsburg, Pennsylvania, printed a two-inch by two-inch pad called a "Complaint Form." In the center of each page was printed a small square, a quarter inch on each side. Above it were the words: "Please write your complaint in Space below. Write Legibly."

A Presbyterian pastor friend of mine passed out these forms to his northeast Pennsylvania congregation. One lady returned it filled. She couldn't put anything more than a vocalized pause in the quarter-inch square, but she filled the rest of the paper, front and back, with complaints. She must have figured that the only way to avoid the temptation to criticize was to yield to it.

Expressions of appreciation and recognition of the positive contributions of others are more effective in creating a climate for consensus and change. Creative change often comes not from being booted but on the heels of commendation. Affirm others genuinely and graciously, rather than constantly harping on their flaws and faults.

One has but to turn to a beaming senior face to recognize that many of them have conquered sour attitudes. They enjoy the Lord's blessings and are full of gratitude, praising His name. Happiness, rather than sourness, radiates from their fragile beings. Instead of complaining, many seniors quietly bite the bullet of hardship. They face their pains with Christian calmness and endurance. They brace themselves and behave thankfully.

WINNING WAYS

• Complaining can become an ingrained habit if it is not nipped in the bud. A sound prevention measure is to discern what is behind or beneath complaints and refuse to be ruled by it.

• A calm submission to what is out of our hands is a common sense—and Christian—approach to disturbing events.

• Bring problems that need fixing to the attention of people who can do something about them.

• Review the preceding eight aspects of complaining and try to make your ways "winning ways." Replace negative impulses with positive responses.

THINGS TO THINK ABOUT:

[1] Complaints are like eggs—some are full of protein, others are rotten and produce sickness. How does one determine what complaints are legitimate, constructive, and healthful?

[2] People lash out when their faults are exposed. Do others complain about us because we are full of flaws, or is it that our good points make them feel inferior? Do some we know find faults in us to make themselves feel better about themselves? Persecution of Christians throughout history was often a backlash to make others' imperfections more tolerable.

[3] Complaining is an awkward and anguishing way to begin dialogue. What good can come from complaints? How can we complain so that alienations are not deepened?

[4] How can a Christian senior not be ambushed by others' complaints and criticism? (One suggestion: Relate to the biblical doctrine of forensic justification, the teaching that Christ's righteousness is given to us and covers us. Read Rom. 8:31-34.)

9

TEMPTED TO GOSSIP

———————◻———————

Morsels on gossip, not gossipy morsels. Here's one from my lecture table:

> Gossip is unsubstantiated tidbits, juiced with fragmented facts, blended with imported interpretations, poured into unsuspecting minds, wrapped around with speculations, and disturbed with over-inflated feelings of being important news.—John Gilmore

> When you don't know why something happened or was decided (e.g. at your church), you invent the why. That's the engine of gossip. Halt it before it becomes a runaway train.[1]—James Qualben

Gossip reveals more about the gossiper than about whomever is its subject. That's one reason it does not make you a good conversationalist. Healthy people don't need to be tattletales. Many of us are natural chatterboxes. But we must be on guard not to engage in picking others apart. Christian encouragement is the art of building up without pulling down. Why do other people's misfortune give gossips their bizarre satisfaction? A person who tingles with news of others' afflictions is doomed to be friendless. What friend would trust a gossip?

Scripture speaks against character assassination (Matt. 5:22; Eph. 4:29, 31; 5:3,4; James 1:26; 1 Tim. 5:13). John Calvin [1509-1564] gave one of the best explanations of gossip's dynamics:

> If others manifest the same endowments we admire in ourselves, or even superior ones, we spitefully belittle and revile these gifts in order to avoid yielding place to such persons. If there are any faults in others, not content with noting them with severe and sharp response, we hatefully exaggerate them. Hence arises such insolence that each one of us, as if exempt from the common lot, wishes to tower above the rest, and loftily and savagely abuses every mortal man, or at least looks down upon him as inferior.[2]

THE MORPHOLOGY OF "GOSSIP"

Gossip delights in reports of the petty, the tawdry, the cheap, and the unfair. The word "gossip" is derived from the Old English *godsibb* or "godparent." In pre-nineteenth-century usage it described warm fellowship between males, not their talk.[3] Later it was used to describe friendly conversation among those awaiting the birth of a child. It was talk, but not of the cheap or vicious variety.

By the nineteenth century, however, it was given a new twist. By then it was used for idle talk, tattling, and back-stabbing insults. Related to "gossip" is our word "anecdote." Anecdote comes from the Greek word *anikdatos*, which is a compound of *anic*, meaning not, and *datos*, meaning published. Something not published was a euphemism for gossip.

Another related word is "trivial." Trivial is from the Latin *trivialis*, which stood for trifling or common gossip. *Trivialis* was made up of the prefix *tri* meaning three combined with *via* meaning road. It described the common chatter of people meeting at a crossroads. The

German *klatch*, as in the familiar coffee *klatch*, has similar roots. Often used in church circles it means, literally, coffee gossip.

DEFINITIONS OF GOSSIP

Gossip is a verbal activity that secretly delights in someone else's supposed fault or failures. In the New Testament there are at least three senses of forbidden speech that relate to gossip.

Non-important Comments—

Jesus warned against idle chatter (Matt. 12:36, 37). In John's Gospel disorderly utterance or mere prattle appears in 4:42 (Greek word: *lalia*).[4] Amidst seemingly inconsequential bantering with the soon-to-be redeemed Samaritan woman, God's good news in Christ got through. The same word was used of Jesus' speech in John 8:43. No matter how plainly Jesus spoke, unbelievers thought he was talking nonsense. Paul met sophisticated gossip mongers on the Areopagus (Acts 17:21).

Rumor—

Neh. 6:6 and Jer. 51:46 mention rumors of no substance. The expression "they said" (*elegon*) in Mark 3:21 also can mean "it was rumored."[5] One first century rumor frightened Christians. It was said that Emperor Nero's suicide (June, '68 A.D.) was false. Although he was publicly buried, a rumor circulated—like Elvis sitings in our day—that Nero had not actually died but was hiding at Parthia. Revelation 13:3 reflects that baseless rumor.

Rumor means the information is slanted and calculated to increase anxiety. Godly persons have been the objects of scurrilous tales. One such was the unsubstantiated rumor that John Bunyan (*Pilgrim's Progress*; seventeenth century) was romantically involved with Agnes Beaumont.[6]

Distinguishing between rumor and fact prompted the publication of Hal Morgan and Kerry Tucker's book *Rumor* (Penguin Books, 1984). Hard-to-believe rumors often get transmitted at face value—even after they have been proven false. One rumor in the 1960s was that a device was invented by MIT and Stanford University that enabled free telephone calls around the world.[7]

In 1982, Cincinnati-based Procter & Gamble did not wait for a book to expose the falsehood in the rumor that the company logo/trademark was a symbol of Satanism and/or devil worship. They spent thousands of dollars, even solicited prominent religious leaders such as Evangelist Billy Graham and the Catholic Cardinal Joseph Bernardin of Chicago, to squelch the rumor.

A woman named Matilda, age eighty-two, who never married, was visited by her pastor. He said, "Matilda, I hear that you are engaged to be married." She replied, "There is not a grain of truth in it, but thank God for the rumor!"

Maligning Character—

Incessant chatter can degenerate into malicious lies. Gossip follows malice (Romans 1:29, NIV) and slander (2 Cor. 12:20, NIV). The most destructive form of gossip maligns character. The prophet Jeremiah, with radar precision, picked up snide comments said about him (Jer. 20:10). The purpose of those comments was to belittle the prophet and reduce or ruin his effectiveness.

The accusation was used against Jesus that He was "talking down" someone. "Talking down" is a literal translation of *antilogian* found in Heb. 12:3, as well as in Luke 2:34; John 19:12; Acts 28:19; Titus 1:9; 2:19; Jude 11. Bishop Westcott's comment was appropriate: "The opposition in words is the beginning of every form and act of opposition."[8]

Accusatory gossip was used against Stephen (Acts

6:10-13) and later against Paul, who likened spreading false insinuations to cancer's rapid growth (2 Tim. 2:17). Although translated as blasphemy in other passages, in Romans 3:8 *blasphemeia* has the sense of something slanderous reported (NIV). *Skleron* in Jude 15, "hard things" (KJV) stands for harsh and disdainful speech (cf. Enoch 101:3). This form of gossip makes others scapegoats and gloats over their alleged missteps. James Packer likened gossip to confessing *other* people's sins.[9] Paul mentioned two persons who maligned Moses by forming a two-some resistance team (2 Tim. 3:8).

GOSSIP OUTLETS

Curiosity about celebrities has created a market for gossip journalism. Shoppers passing through food market checkout lanes see tabloids with the latest gossip about Hollywood stars. Let's "fess up." Some seniors are gossips. It may happen via telephone tongue-wagging that tries to bridge the outside world and workplace where once watercooler gossip was common. A person accustomed to shop talk, locker room chatter, and coffee-table scuttlebutt find it hard to give up an insatiable need for petty news. In retirement three basic gossip devices are at our disposal: tabloids, television, and the telephone.

Admittedly, gossip may be a source of relaxation and entertainment for some, but one dubiously attractive feature of gossip is that it requires no intellectual skills. It has no morally nutritious value; it is essentially conversational junk food. Gossip spreads hearsay as fact. It is tempting to listen to, even tempting to repeat, but its impact is negative.

IS GOSSIP A PREDOMINANTLY FEMALE FAULT?

In the seventh century, an Irish saint named Columbanus included in his penitential manual lists of sinful offenders, women who engaged in gossip while pretending to pray.[10] John Milton [1608-1674] furthered a sexist stereo-typing of women by writing in his poem, "Samson Agonistes"—

> Curiosity, inquisitive, importune
> Of secrets, then with like infirmity
> To publish them—both common female faults.

I believe the assumption women are more gossipy than men is itself a false rumor. For a Louella Parsons we had a Walter Winchell, for a Hedda Hopper there was a Drew Pearson, for a Janet Charlton there was a Cleveland Amory. I find it interesting that the Bible does not identify falsehood with either sex. The need to guard one's speech is not directed against one segment of society, but all persons regardless of gender.

The biblical record of bad-mouthing males is well-known, especially the erroneous conclusions of Job's three male friends. That should be enough—in Christian circles—to mute males maligning women. Throughout the history of damaging gossip against Christianity, one finds men were at the forefront of false rumors and innuendo. During the Early Church era, examples include Trypho, Celsus, and Arius.

We cannot divide along gender lines such as the contentions that "debate is masculine and conversation is feminine." If one were to judge the right-vs.-wrong of this statement, the contention would die, although some women today would assume men have an edge in debate.

Is Gossip a Temptation for Retirees?

Gossip lends itself to those who have a lot of time on their hands. The expression "idle gossips" should never have been invented because some people we know seem to work at it at least twelve hours a day. Many seniors are not bothered by fear of reprisal from anyone. Too many assume they don't have to worry that spreading falsehood will jeopardize their relationships.

But leisure time can be at the root of seniors' temptation to gossip. Whether in business or organizations, access to "inside" information is a measure of how much power one has. Upon retirement, most insiders are cut off from such information. That void draws retirees to keep up their trivia collection by gossiping. A power void with a need for "inside information" inspires gossip in the stream of conversation.

Seniors suffer from false gossip about their capabilities, inclinations, abilities, and interests. For example, isn't it gossip plain and simple that anyone past sixty-five is a "has been"? With at least one-third of their lives ahead of them, however, many seniors can make significant contributions to various organizations and disciplines. As far back as Abraham one finds that "incapacities" in advanced age have been distorted. Abram tried to correct the damage of this false gossip throughout the land: That "the King of Sodom made Abram rich" (Gen. 14:23). God was concerned that Israel's cohesiveness not be jeopardized by tale-bearing (Lev. 19:16-18). Wisdom advised banning unsupported tidbits of scandalous information. Proverbs 26:20, NIV, says, "Without wood a fire goes out; without gossip a quarrel dies down."

SATAN, GOSSIP'S PROMOTER

Satan is the arch gossip. He fathers falsehoods and circulates them throughout the cosmos. The "accuser of the brethren" (Rev. 12:10) is devoted to disparaging Christians night and day. But gossip is the least sophisticated means by which the image, reputation, and morale of Christians can be negatively affected. Satan specializes outright lies and murder (John 8:44).

Several years ago "Nobody's Friend" appeared in a Sunday bulletin of Tenth Presbyterian Church in Philadelphia, PA. It gave the following description of gossip.

> My name is Gossip. I have no respect for justice.
> I maim without killing. I break hearts and ruin lives.
> I am cunning and malicious and gather strength with age.
> The more I am quoted the more I am believed.
> My victims are helpless.
> They cannot protect themselves against me,
> because I have no name and no face.
> To track me down is impossible.
> The harder you try, the more elusive I become.
>
> I am nobody's friend.
> Once I tarnish a reputation, it is never the same.
> I topple governments and wreck marriages.
> I ruin careers and cause sleepless nights, heartache and
>   indigestion.
> I make innocent people cry in their pillows.
> Even my name hisses.
> I am called Gossip.
> I make headlines and headaches.[11]

False friends slander. One of Satan's names is "slanderer." (*Diabolou* is translated "devil," the slanderer.) Judas Iscariot slandered Jesus—"One of you is a slanderer [Devil]!" (John 6:70). "A gossip betrays a confidence" (Prov. 11:3, NIV). Judas betrayed the hiding place of Jesus during Passover. Judas also scorned Jesus' agenda and slandered our Lord's intentions, values, and mission when he hoped Jesus would lead Israel's revolution against Roman rule.

Satan has a gossip's predilection for taking half-truth information out of context. Gossips are experts at using half-truths to ruin someone else's reputation in order to justify their own—usually worse—behavior.

When Satan quoted from the book of Deuteronomy, he applied the passages out of context and twisted Scripture. But Jesus did not fall for his use of titles and texts. Jesus' insistence that Scripture be honored as divine self-revelation and not as a tool for personal gain stood out when He reminded Satan of the totality and finality of the revelation: "It is written" (Matt. 4:4,7,10). Satan wanted Jesus to take advantage of His relationship with the Father. But Jesus resisted that and solely relied on divine revelation.

Satan tried to treat Jesus' relationship with the Father, angels, and with this world as fictional unless *proven*. This showed Satan's alienation from the material he professed to handle with such precision and politeness. Satan revealed he is an arch gossip in that he was less concerned about the total picture's accuracy than about the advantage he might gain by manipulating fragments of Scripture. (Beware, even now, of those who use pious "Bible Speak" to gain their own advantage!)

But Jesus came back with passages that kept the biblical balance—"it is written again." When Satan quoted a segment of Scripture out of context, Jesus both challenged and countered his misuse of Scripture.

Although Jesus overcame Satan's distortion of Scripture, the general population fell for anti-Christ gossip that circulated during His public ministry. Mary, Jesus' mother, also must have felt the pain of gossip about her son's birth. Simeon anticipated the same fate for Jesus (Luke 2:34). Later, Jesus would anticipate gossip against His followers (Matt. 5:11). He challenged false gossip about the moral condition of those who met an untimely death when a tower toppled and struck workmen (Luke 13:4).

Gossip gouged Jesus' image long before His last week. For example, rumor had it that Jesus suffered from paranoia (Mark 3:21). Jesus' extended relatives seemed to have bought into this rumor. His own family, though "...they did not originate the charge, they gave credence to it and acted upon it."[12]

Gossip played a role in precipitating Jesus' arrest, trial, and death.[13] His misunderstood statement about the Temple was later used as condemning evidence of His supposed blasphemy (John 2:19; Mark 14:58). Christ's words regarding the Temple were twisted twice (Matt. 26:61 [Mk. 14:57,58]; Acts 6:14). "Inside scoop" about Jesus' alleged negative attitude toward the Temple was really an "outside suggestion" coming from His implacable foe, Satan.

Curiosity can turn into a compulsion to judge others. Knowing something secret about someone seems to feed our sense of importance. Information about a person can make us feel we have power over that person's life and destiny. If we never had fame (or notoriety), a kind of celebrity comes from being among those who are "in the know."

Ironically, the gossip who can so freely judge others is himself afraid of being judged.[14] From that perspective, gossip becomes a technique by which a fragile ego lifts its sense of self-importance. Helmut Thielicke commented: "We want our own superiority to be confirmed, and we achieve this by being horrified at others and putting ourselves above them."[15] This should be a warning to us about what we reveal about ourselves when we gossip. Whenever we fret over what others think of us, we are tempted to create gossip, collect it, repeat it.

What is Gossip? What is Not?

Electronic eavesdropping—including tapped telephones —are now stringently regulated. However, the criteria remain fuzzy: What constitutes truth and lies, fact and fiction, opinion and reality, conjecture and truth. Trying to turn gossip into fact is the agenda of those who intend to hurt someone.

Gossip becomes a profession whenever we want to paste the "Guilty" label on another for criminal, punishable, or—most often— immoral behavior. Many of us quite innocently pick up fragmentary information and repeat it. Do we know how to distinguish gossip from appropriate information? Here are some suggestions:

[1] *Ask how the person telling you something learned of it.*

Does he or she have direct first-hand knowledge of what is reported or is it hearsay? Hearsay is second-hand information liable to distortion and misinformation. Exodus 23:1 (Moffatt) says, "You must never repeat a baseless rumor."

[2] *Are there witnesses?*

The Bible insists that accusations be confirmed by at least two or three witnesses. In Scripture there is no "witness protection" program, but there is a protection insured by witnesses. Witnesses were required to confirm a statement or event (Deut. 17:6).

[3] *How well known is the person reporting?*

Repeating news is not necessarily playing gossip. If that were always the case, then Gabriel telling Mary about Elizabeth's pregnancy would amount to angelic gossip (Luke 1:36,37). Gabriel knew the information was not hearsay, because he was the one who had told Zechariah about his wife's approaching pregnancy (Luke 1:13f). Paul was able to keep abreast of what was happening in various local churches through reliable couriers. Tychicus went to Colossae to discover the state of affairs there (Col. 4:7). Chloe reported to Paul on the condition of Corinthian Christians (1 Cor. 1:11). She discovered and disclosed their schism. It was not that she was pleased to report their divisions, but she felt Paul should know what had happened in his absence. Paul did not regard the information as inflated or distorted. He knew Chole was a conscientious informant, not a troubled fomenter of bad news bent on inflating her own importance.

How does one distinguish between information that warrants wider circulation, especially to individuals in a position of leadership, and whether it should be allowed to die? This is a difficult question. We should ask ourselves three standard questions: Is it kind? Is it verifiable? Is it necessary? A good rule is never to report something that may hurt someone else unless a still greater hurt to others will result from concealing it.[16]

[4] *Bad news is potentially capable of great harm.*

You know you're about to be jolted with a shocker when a person begins, "I'm not one to repeat gossip, so listen carefully the first time." Tragic consequences have followed baseless stories. We should never gleefully hear or glibly repeat information about others' moral failures. Not only may one individual be unjustly maligned, but whole families and careers could be destroyed. This outcome was noted in Proverbs 16:28 (NIV)—"A perverse man stirs up dissension, and a gossip separates close friends." And therein lies another purpose of gossip: To cut another off from his or her friends and, hopefully, co-opt them for oneself.

The Apostle Paul spoke out strongly against gossips. The practice of gossip was considered by Paul to be one mark of a non-Christian (Rom. 1:29; 2 Cor. 12:20). Just how serious the sin of distorting another person's character becomes clear in the Pauline warning that malicious slander keeps one out of heaven (1 Cor. 5:10; 6:10)!

> If you heard a bit of gossip
> Whether false or whether true,

Be it of a friend or stranger,
Let me tell you what to do.
Button up your lips securely.
Lest the tale you should repeat,
And bring sorrow into someone
Whose life now is not too sweet.
If you know of one who yielded
To temptation long ago,
But whose life has since been blameless,
Let me tell you what to do.
Button up your lips securely,
His the secret: God alone
Has the right to sit in judgment,
Treat it as to you unknown.

Sometimes life is filled with troubles,
Oft its burdens are severe,
Do not make it any harder
By a careless word or sneer.
Button up your lips securely
Gainst the words that bring a tear,
But be swift with words of comfort
Words of praise and words of cheer.
—Author Unknown[17]

TALKING UP INSTEAD OF TALKING DOWN

Psalm 11:2 (NIV) gives an apt description of gossips: "They shoot from the shadows." True Christian fellowship does not tear people down. It talks *up* the Faith, the Christian cause, and builds up the Body of Christ. It shares the gospel in the context of daily life.

The Christian heart is best known by what it tempers or improves, not by what it finds tempting or impoverishing. The wayward do need occasional admonition or correction (Neh. 9:30, NIV), but the wavering and weak also need frequent encouragement (Heb. 12:3, 12). Mutual exhortation is a mark of true Christianity (Phil. 2:1; 4:2; I Thess. 4:1). Christian concern does not tell people where to get off, but how to get back on. That is why the Christian neither puts *on* nor puts *down*. The story Christians should most delight to hear and to tell is the "old, old story, of Jesus and His love."

Old man Job had remarkable people skills. Elephaz complimented Job: "Your words keep men on their feet" (Job 4:4, Moffatt). John Foxe's *Acts and Monuments of matters happening in the Church* (1563), commonly known as *Foxe's Book of Martyrs*, described a second-century Christian woman named Blandina who encouraged another to stay true to Christ during the persecutions under Marcus Aurelius (162 AD). Ponticus, a young man of fifteen, was strengthened by Blandina and was able to hold to his convictions in the face of impending death. He died a faithful martyr.

John Bunyan wrote in his autobiography, *Grace Abounding*, of Bedford washer women who discussed the Christian gospel rather than run down their neighbors. Bunyan was powerfully motivated toward belief in Christ by their sincere personal expressions of faith.[18] Gospel, not gossip, should be the first news from our lips, for by it the hearts of men are given hope in the Lord.

Christ enables us to see potential for God's grace in lives where others only notice flaws. Recovery of the fallen is the purpose of Christian witness. Therefore, telling others the good news of God's gracious love in Christ is a prime means by which lives are transformed. Awareness of our own pardon in Christ frees us to acknowledge others' needs for it.

Whereas gossip divides people, the gospel begins, unites, and cements relationships. The gospel draws people to the centrality of Christ. The glorious gospel of Christ is the instrument God has ordained to make and nurture the church. Without the gospel, expressions of gratitude to others can degenerate to pride-building transactions.

If with pleasure you are viewing any work a man is doing,
If you like him or you love him, tell him now.
Don't withhold your approbation till the parson makes oration
As he lies with snowy lilies o'er his brow;
For no matter how you shout it, he won't really care about it;
He won't know how many teardrops you have shed.
If you think some praise is due him,
Now's the time to slip it to him;
For he cannot read his tombstone when he's dead!

More than fame and more than money is the comment kind and sunny
And a hearty warm approval of a friend;
For it gives to life a savor, and it makes you stronger, braver,
And it gives you heart and spirit to the end;
If he hears your praise, bestow it;
If you like him let him know it;
Let the words of true encouragement be said;
Do not wait till life is over and he's underneath the clover,
For he cannot read his tombstone when he is dead.
—Author Unknown[19]

WINNING WAYS

• Keep your speech constructive, not destructive.

• Avoid repeating unsubstantiated speculations.

• Check your speech at all times. David wanted a guard over his tongue and asked God to be that guard.

• When someone offers you "information" about another, ask yourself: What is its purpose?

THINGS TO THINK ABOUT:

[1] Distinguish between factual reporting and gossip. Do you see differences between gossip and story? Would gossip die without a ready listener? As listeners, what can we do to discourage gossip?

[2] Give some examples from the Bible of how public reputation did not define the person's true relationship with God. Who in the Bible had a squeaky-clean reputation, yet was a dissembling, dangerous person? Who in the Bible was considered trash, but God put them in faith's Hall of Fame (e.g. Hebrews 11)?

[3] False accusations and supposed guilt have often been proven wrong throughout history. If a person's true condition were to be judged by public consensus, how would Christ have rated in His lifetime? How did Paul's attitude toward Stephen change (see Acts 7)?

[4] Gossip widens chasms between people. How did Christ expect grudges to be settled (see Matt. 18:15-20)? How should one handle the person eager to share a derogatory piece of news?

10

TEMPTED TO BE BULLHEADED

───────◼───────

...old age is a kind of detector, a magnifying glass which shows up the tendencies that have been there over a long period....The kindly person becomes more so as he advances in age. The critical person now never stops grumbling....[1]—Paul Tournier

Bullheaded is a derogatory and unflattering adjective. To suggest seniors are especially prey to bullheadedness is a snap judgement. And to insist that mature adults are more tempted to it than others is itself bullheaded thinking.

At the outset, we face three questions: [1] What is bullheadedness? [2] Are seniors any more bullheaded than other groups? and [3] If bullheadedness is so bad, how can it also be a temptation?

WHAT IS BULLHEADEDNESS?

The British phrase "bloody-mindedness" may be a richer term than bullheadedness. Bloody-mindedness includes an overtone of persistence in a worthy cause. Bullheadedness, however, implies a stubborn refusal to back off from a bad decision.

A person who can't see important surrounding issues is said to suffer from "tunnel vision." Tunnel vision
that lasts and deepens hampers happiness and allows
hang-ups to hold us back. A person with tunnel vision
may not charge like a bull, but his goals are narrowly
focused.

Consumers with blind loyalty to a certain product
brand illustrate bullheadedness. Brand-loyal customers
proverbially refuse to switch or try alternative products. A consumer, however, need not be a customer. For
example, nursing home residents continue to eat, but
they don't continue to shop for food. But even at that
stage of life and out of sheer bullheadedness, a person
can refuse to eat what is prepared.

ARE SENIORS ESPECIALLY BULLHEADED?

Three O's are not all "cheerie": Orneriness, Obstinacy,
and Outspokenness.

Outspokenness, of course, can result from a transparent honesty. But how can honesty keep its honor when
it cohabits with bullheadedness?

Most seniors would prefer to be considered honest
more than smart. We value integrity more than brains.
We prefer to be known as always straightforward rather
than always right. As one ages there is less and less
desire to keep up pretenses. Retirees find it easier to
resist a—

> —bargain they can't use
> —product they don't like
> —style they can't wear
> —joke they don't get
> —spree they can't afford
> —rumor they can't swallow
> —candidate they can't support.

ARE MIDDLE-AGED FOLKS AS BULLHEADED?

Closed minds do not emerge at a certain age. Open and closed minds are found in all age groups. It is not true that most seniors have one-track minds. Many seniors are capable of moving along multiple routes for mental travel than those half their age.

But hardened attitudes can kill happiness as effectively as hardened arteries kill people! Stretch is a rubber-band quality that God wants Christian seniors to show. Hopefully, as we age we retain some of the flexibility usually associated with youth.

Rigidity, however, is not confined to seniors. If you find seniors whose attitudes are rigid, chances are good that they were rigid in younger years. Equally so, a flexible youth is likely to carry that flexibility into senior years.

An eighty-four-year-old woman from Seattle, Washington wrote to *The Seattle Times:*

> As the cells in my body renew
> And my purpose in life I review,
> I find, growing older,
> I'm now growing bolder
> And increasingly hard to subdue. [2]

Have you a friend secretly grieving over capabilities slipping away? Tim Stafford in *As Our Years Increase* told of a nursing home resident who always insisted that her coffee cup only be half filled. She got attention, he speculated, by trying to escape the impersonality of eating in a cafeteria.[3] Sickness can make us negative, even nasty, blunt, gruff, and brusque. Our reaction to delayed recovery may be irritability. When a person reaches an advanced stage of dependency on others, his requests can sound like barks; his remarks may seem bellowed instead of calmly stated. But be reminded: sharp words usually show *distress* rather than *dislike.*

Obstinacy at any age indicates fear—fear of change, especially. Apprehension makes us stubborn. Unfamiliar settings, such as going to a hospital, can frighten a person, young or old. When a senior's poor health compels him to enter assisted living quarters, it is a reluctant move. This option usually is unwelcome, because it seems a threat to freedom.

Nobody likes to be institutionalized. If adult children pressure parents to sell their home, the parents may refuse because they feel the decision is being forced upon them rather than being an outcome of extended mutual consultation. Seniors often resist losing driving privileges. How would you feel if told your driving license can't be renewed even though you know that your poor eyesight means your driving puts others at risk. Freedom of movement is hard to surrender.

Simone de Beauvoir was convinced seniors are preoccupied and obsessed with ownership. She held that the elderly transferred "who they are" to "what they own." Their possessions become part of their person. Their possessions become their reason for being. For this reason "the old person very much dislikes having his things used or even touched by others."[4]

Can Bullheadedness Be a Temptation?

Bullheadedness is a negative trait. But bullheadedness, like bossiness, is a temptation *because* it can masquerade as commendable. My "courage of conviction" may be your stubbornness. No one sees himself as bullheaded, inflexible, cantankerous, and rigid. An eighty-year-old man may not think himself old. His mind may not be mixed-up, but it may be permanently set like concrete.

How does one distinguish between principled conviction and cantankerousness, between Christian steadfastness and ungodly bullheadedness? Firm loyalty to the Lord is a mark of sainthood. And persistence in pursuit of a hunt can pay off. Staying on one's course can yield rich dividends. If Englishman Howard Carter and his patron, Lord Carnarvon, were not so obstinate in 1922, they would have abandoned seeking the prize that eluded Egyptologists for centuries, the tomb of the boy king Tutankhamun.

Perseverance in faith and obedience are features of genuine Christianity. We applaud those who follow Christ wholeheartedly. Fidelity to Christ against odds and opposition is a mark of Christian faithfulness.

Polycarp (ca. AD 69-155), bishop of Smyrna, was an exemplary Christian. His refusal to honor Caesar's deity before a Roman proconsul was accompanied by his famous confession:

> I have been Christ's servant for eighty-six years, and he has done me no wrong. How then can I blaspheme my King who saved me?" [When threatened with being devoured by wild beasts or burned alive Polycarp continued]...You threaten that fire which burns for a season and after a little while is quenched; for you are ignorant of the fire of the future judgment and eternal punishment which is reserved for the ungodly.[5]

Paul deplored fickleness in faith. "So that we may no longer be children, tossed to and fro and carried about with every wind of doctrine, by the cunning of men, by their craftiness in deceitful wiles" (Ephesians 4:14, RSV). Our spiritual resolve includes holding fast to the Word of truth (Titus 1:9). Only a permissive age would heap scorn on those who stand for eternal principles. If that seems like bullheadedness, such is a bulwark of the church.

Bullheadedness is a frozen prejudice, a persistent mind-set of rejection. Although some would castigate fidelity to law and gospel as regressive rigidity and a cultural anachronism, we know that unflappable adherence to Christ and His Word is essential.

A person hardened in bullheaded unbelief will reject the authority of Scripture in favor of the latest cultural fads. But unswerving firmness in the confession of Christ is beneficial both now and later (Heb. 10:23). Both the non-Christian and Christian can demonstrate commitment, firmness, and determination—but in different directions.

BULLHEADEDNESS CAN BE
BENEFICIAL AND BENEVOLENT

Thank God for the Bill of Rights and our judicial system. Overhauling outdated or decrepit institutions and process is a task that requires steadfastness in seeking justice.

Health care operations can slide into unsafe and unsanitary states without firm adherence to professional standards. Dehumanizing conditions in nursing homes must be caught, challenged, and corrected. When that doesn't happen, when state inspectors are bribed or look the other way, and when nursing home owners accuse whistle-blowing employees of "bullheaded legalism," residents are put at risk.

We rightly demand state inspectors willing to slap hefty penalties on any dangerous facilities. We want state inspectors stubbornly insistent on compliance for the welfare of residents. Certification and rectification procedures must not be relaxed or ignored. Violators must be closely and critically monitored for reoccurrences. Any noncompliance should be grounds for shutting down a facility.

BULLHEADED FROM BELOW?

We might not understand why others interpret our loyalties as inflexibility. Psychological counseling has done a valuable service in helping us understand the dynamics of denial, compensation, projection, and re-pression—four major ways we cope in threatening situations, ways that can come off as "bullheaded." Why do people freeze up? Why do they resist change? The bottom line is that stubbornness can become a cover-up for unfulfilled and unrecognized feelings. When we are bullheaded, we hide a realization that our position is weak.

Bullheadedness can be a form of deeply-seated aggressive behavior. Overly aggressive people express their insecurity. A person who conveys illusions of confidence may be filled with uncertainties. An obnoxiously authoritarian person projects the feeling he is indifferent toward acceptance when, in fact, his demands crave acceptance. His craving for closeness and acceptance can be repressed under a veneer of dogmatism.

IS BULLHEADEDNESS SATANICALLY INSPIRED?

Scripture devotes lots of space to a condition rarely noticed today. Spiritual stubbornness is a major subject in both Old and New Testaments. Hosea said, "The Israelites are stubborn like a stubborn heifer" (4:16, NIV). Israel's hardened spiritual attitude also got repeated notice in Old Testament Psalms (Pss. 75:5; 81:11, 12). Israel sought to include experimental variations of pagan worship, in defiance of Scripture. They refused to give up their evil practices (Judges 2:19). The prophet Jeremiah attacked their stubborn preference for evil thinking and behavior (Jer. 5:3,4,23, 24; 7:24; 9:13, 14; 17:23; 18:12; 23:17).

Throughout the New Testament, Satan inspired resistance to the gospel. In Jesus' three wilderness temptations, Satan began with assumptions about his own stature. In the first temptation, he hid his unflagging, unbending rejection of Jesus' claim to be divine and implied that he would embrace his claims if Jesus would repeat the miracle of manna. In temptations two and three, Satan never let on that he was stubbornly committed to foiling Jesus' later redemptive activity.

Strange as it may seem, Satan also tempted Jesus through a callused Jewish audience. Sanhedrinists required hard physical evidence that Christ was the Messiah (Mark 8:11-12)—a "sign"—which Jesus saw as a satanic demand. In Mark's Gospel, however, "the only true sign is the cross which paradoxically is both a tragedy of outward defeat and a revelation of who Jesus really is."[6]

The rebuff of Jesus' authority was due to Satan's activity. Jesus' preaching was often met with apathy, and at heart that indifference was deliberate satanic defiance.

> [Jesus] looked around at them in anger and, deeply distressed at their stubborn hearts, said to the man [with the shriveled hand], 'Stretch out your hand.' He stretched it out, and his hand was completely restored. Then the Pharisees went out and began to plot with the Herodians how they might kill Jesus. (Mark 3:5,6 NIV)

At both ends of our Lord's life were two elderly men— Herod "the Great" and the High Priest Annas—who demonstrated both entrenched rejection and self-importance. The ages of both these men can be calculated from contemporary documents outside the New Testament.

Herod the Great—

When Christ was born, Herod the Great was not only near the end of his reign, he was near the end of his life. Flavius Josephus [377-100 AD], the Jewish historian, tells us that Herod died near age seventy, March or April, 4 BC. (The probable year of Jesus' birth, since

Dionysus Exiguus [6th century] miscalculated the calendar.) He was a senior, but he was not the kind we would want to know or one with whom we would care to have a disagreement.

Herod was a barbarian at heart, yet he promoted cultural and civic improvement programs. After all, he rebuilt the Temple. The last nine years of his reign were marked by family discord and criminal plots (13-4 BC).[7] Capacity for spiritual rebellion does not disappear when one becomes older.

When Herod sought the birth place of the newborn king, he consulted Old Testament experts, but insincerely. He wanted to destroy Jesus, not worship him. Herod had no intention of exerting himself by a two or three hour trip to Bethlehem to worship Jesus. He listened to news about Jesus, not that he might more accurately seek Him but that he might more certainly destroy Him. Herod was not interested in Jesus as the Messiah because he jealously feared that his own title, "King of the Jews," was in jeopardy.

Annas the High Priest—

At the other end of Jesus' life was Annas, a retired High Priest, the shadowy influence guiding his son-in-law Joseph Caiaphas in Jesus' trial. Annas was wealthy, wily, wicked—and old! He headed Judaism's supreme court from 6 to 15 AD, but he continued to exert influence over the Sanhedrin after he left office. Although retired from the highest office of Judaism, Annas was highly respected, feared, and followed. His title masked his moral corruption. He was *officially* retired, but not *emotionally* so. Indeed, he actively conspired in Jesus' death (John 18:13).

Annas' last major ambition was to rid Judaism of Jesus. Annas considered Jesus a threat to his economic interests in overcharging pilgrims for sacrificial animals.[8] When Jesus cleansed the Temple, first at the start of His ministry and again at the end of it, Annas found personal grounds to have Jesus crucified.

Annas reminds us that though Herod the Great was gone, Satan can recruit respected religious retirees to carry out his opposition to Christ, employing every legal loophole, engine, and influence possible to discredit Jesus and destroy Him. Both Herod the Great and Annas are examples of the worst sort of bullheaded living.

UNBELIEF IN PEOPLE OF EVERY AGE

Nowhere is human stubbornness more evident than in spurning God's gift of eternal life in Christ.

> The heart that does not want to be fortified through grace, fortifies itself against God, becomes hardened and stubborn, and refuses to hear or see anything divine, but all the same in the last resort fumes against itself.[9]

There is a streak in everyone of us that refuses to abandon habituated reactions. The heart is not cured with age. We never outgrow our carnal inclinations: "The carnal mind is enmity against God; it is not subject to the law of God, neither indeed can it be" (Romans 8:7-8 KJV). Tragically, opposition to the gospel doesn't weaken with age.

> Once we hold God's Word in contempt, we shake off all reverence for him. For, unless we listen attentively to him, his majesty will not dwell among us, nor his worship remain perfect[10]

Opposition to God arises not from aging alone, but out of our natural alienation from God. Resistance to the gospel of Christ roots in contempt. It is "a brazen obduracy and contemptible stiff-headedness."[11]

WHAT ABOUT CHRISTIAN SENIORS?

The Bible balances those two surly seniors—Herod the Great and Annas—with two prominent Old Testament patriarchs whose hearts were tender toward God— Isaac and Jacob.

First, Isaac was confident he was confirming the birthright on Esau, his first born, when in fact he was tricked into thinking he was blessing Esau. But Jacob received Isaac's blessing as much from Isaac's rigid loyalty to tradition as from blunder. Isaac was 137 years old. He would not rescind his blessing on Jacob (we know from Genesis 37:1-40). He had no option of recanting.

Ironically, Genesis tells of another senior act of stubbornness, but this time it had to do with Jacob. Jacob, just before he died (over 130 years of age), repeated the stubborn act of his father, Isaac.

> When Joseph saw his father [Jacob] placing his right hand on Ephraim's head he was displeased; so he took hold of his father's hand to move it from Ephraim's head to Manasseh's head. Joseph said to him, 'No, my father, this one is the firstborn; put your right hand on his head.' But his father refused and said, 'I know, my son, I know. He too will become a people, and he too will become great. Nevertheless, his younger brother will be greater than he, and his descendants will become a group of nations. (Gen. 48:17-19 NIV)

Offsetting these Old Testament examples of stubborn old age is the example of noble Abraham. At three junctures in his life, though old, Abraham showed remarkable flexibility and openness to new directions.

[1] *Abraham's Call*—

When Abram migrated from Ur of the Chaldees, he was seventy-five years old (Gen. 12:4). Leaving a prosperous family life in a familiar land might lead others to back off and stay put. Who at seventy-five likes to pick up stakes and enter a foreign land (unless it is the "good old USA") to begin a new life? Maybe your parents as adult immigrants did just that.

[2] *Abraham's Circumcision*—

When God told him to be circumcised, Abraham was ninety-nine years old (Gen. 17:11, 12). He could have tried to beg off, but he didn't (17:25). He didn't say, "Why bother?" Abraham did not give the snappy reply, "Not on your life!" He was willing to obey God again, honor the covenant sanction and submit to the knife. Abraham's openness rebuked stubbornness.

Abraham's reaction was understandable as commentator George Bush [1796-1858] noted: It is one of the temptations of old age to be tenacious of what we have...and to find excuses from being exempted from hard and dangerous duties.[12] But Abraham overcame that instinctive resistance to God's command.

[3] *Abraham's Call to Sacrifice Isaac*—

When God called Abram to offer up his only son, Abraham was over one hundred years old (Gen. 21:4). Abraham believed God and did not try to talk God out of it. The story of Abraham's obedience to God (Genesis 22) stops us from accepting wet-blanket generalizations that stubbornness always goes with old age.

Godly compliance is illustrated in the book of Acts. Flexibility about mission targets was a major apostolic era controversy. One segment, the Jerusalem Christians (mostly believing Jews) were of the opinion that the mission field was to be confined to Jews. Greek-speaking Jews saw the need for reaching others, including the Gentiles. Stephen (Acts 7) represented the later faction who were more outward bound in their mission goals.

"The local Jerusalem Christians...had little thought of going out with the gospel; if anything they expected Diaspora Jews and heathen to come to them, to worship in the temple in the end time."[13]

Mission flexibility still embroils aging and ancient denominations. Those frustrated by a programmatic status quo should want to drop ineffective strategies and try something new. Bureaucratic bullheadedness toward methodological diversity can cause Christ's vineyard to shrink its influence as it shirks its duty to use appropriate means. "We have never done that before" has become the epitaph of dead churches.

> Mental flexibility encourages a spirit of openness and growth in old age, while mental rigidity seems to be associated with intellectual stagnation and eventual withdrawal.[14]

Diversity in approach is healthy, progressive, and shows conquest over fear of change. Churches needlessly suffer loss from rigidity in how they do mission and ministry. Sticks thrown into well-directed ecclesiastical wheels only make progress more difficult. The Christian Church is a senior institution—it has been around a long time. Innovative approaches to outreach do not mean it has necessarily abandoned the core of the gospel.

Admittedly, institutional ruts can distract from a church's progressive image. On the other hand, beneath resistance to valid change instability usually lurks. A destabilized church rarely realizes it is. And at the root of such instability is confusion over Identity.

The Christian church is like a kite in the wind because it is both held and yet free to move. Churches become powerless to grow when they have lost either the knowledge of who they are, what they are about—in Christ— and why, or the willingness to risk their kite to the winds.

Two Observations

Berkouwer observes that the fear of accommodation to changed times and to changing human insight has often led to petrifaction. Similarly, Lyle Schaller notes that the more rigid the organizational or bureaucratic structure, the greater the resistance to innovation.

One sensible principle of church growth is to put aside ineffective habits, attempt new methods and organize fresh programs. Thankfully, the early church overcame programmatic rigor mortis. Richard Lovelace noted:

> If the apostolic church had failed to take the steps described in Acts 10-15, its spread among the nations would have stopped dead, and the power of God would have been withdrawn from its inner life.[15]

How to Tell if Your Congregation is Bullheaded

We have to test our attitudes before we should seek to alter them. Take a moment to score yourselves on cooperation and critical self-evaluation. Before productive congregational changes can take place, we must examine our attitudes. Thankfully, members are usually far more progressive and sensible as individuals than they are in church decision-making settings. Blessings upon Christ's corporate body require a willingness to adapt, adjust, and be creative. David O. Moberg has written, "Once a program has been adopted, it must be flexible enough to change with the changing needs of a changing world. There can be no fixed 'Christian status quo' in modern society."[16]

Egocentricity often feeds ecclesiastical rigidity. Attitude is what makes or breaks a person, a program, or an institution. We are flexible where we find a variety of willing attitudes.

Here are seven areas where we can measure our potential for change:

—a willingness to discuss mission options (most churches were originally mission minded. Some lose that as they age.)

—a willingness to re-examine our criteria for judging and decision-making.

—a willingness to weigh motivational dynamics.

—a willingness to evaluate relational ramifications of decisions such as motives and purposes.

—a willingness to revise proven ineffective agenda.

—a willingness to be realistic about personal investment.

—a willingness to stretch in directions never attempted.

We know what kills humans. We know what kills churches. For churches and seniors alike, the difference between a rut and a grave can be only a matter of inches.

But wannabe "change agents" also have to realize that successful change won't happen if attempts shun continuity with the organization's heritage. That is why, for example, no successful revolution has ever been led by a radical—someone who hasn't "paid his dues" in the system he wants to change. When the leader of change is perceived as a steward of its core heritage, the congregation tends to follow.

The Welsh preacher Daniel Rowland [1771-1790] said that in old age he wanted to learn four lessons:

—to repent without despairing;
—to believe without presuming;
—to rejoice without levity;
—to be angry without sinning.[17]

Four other goals can be added for modern seniors:

—to be firm without being rigid
—to be flexible without being spineless
—to be analytical without being apathetic
—to be concerned without being anxious.

WINNING WAYS

• Our bodies may be frail, but our attitudes can be well exercised. Resistance to change can be good or it can be evil. Compare and scrutinize either outcome with Scriptural examples.

• Employ the tests of bullheadedness cited near the end of this chapter.

• Evaluate any apparent need for change "transgenerationally;" that is, as to how accountable it is to both predecessors and successors.

• Pray for guidance in all your decision making.

THINGS TO THINK ABOUT:

[1] Take the phrases—
        I am firm
        He is obstinate
        They are pigheaded.
In light of this chapter, how does each phrase reflect human nature?

[2] Ideological hardness can lead to relational harshness. Read Colossians 3:12. What does this verse have to say to how we approach people and our responses in a group?

[3] Identify a recent example of dedication to principle that faced strong institutional opposition but had a decisive influence for the better.

[4] Adamant adherence to petty rules characterizes the apparatus of both cultic and plateaued organizations. Consider the effects of such legalism on Christian churches' attitudes and lack of confidence in the Gospel.

11

TEMPTED TO
SELF-PITY

Senator Strom Thurmond, at age 93 and over six feet tall, radiates confidence. He is a great advertisement against self-pity and pining common among some seniors. In 1996, in Summerville, SC, at a political gathering, those who shook his hand felt a powerful grip. In response to the shock he saw on their faces, he apologized explaining that it was the result of years of weight lifting. "I watch my diet and I get exercise." Instead of moaning about body aches Strom Thurmond, who embodies heartiness, paid tribute to the benefits of self-discipline, and the worthlessness of self-pity.[1]

Yielding to the temptation to self-pity in aging only enhances self-defeat and contributes to increased weakness.

It is difficult to rank this temptation by frequency and severity for two reasons:

- We age at different rates, and different ages can have distinct temptations.
- Each of us obviously varies in our ability to resist specific temptations.

Loneliness intrudes on individuals in various forms. Yet it is a major temptation. And few seniors escape self-pity. Single adults learn to confront this all through life. For instance, after many years of marriage, those deprived of a spouse can find their introduction to this problem quite intense. For those divorced or widowed, loneliness is a recurring temptation.

When others avoid, neglect, forget, and don't spend time with us, we can feel isolated, alienated, rejected. This was illustrated by a letter in "Dear Abby."

> Dear Abby: I am a 79-year-old widow. I have been alone for 17 years, with no love or help from anyone....I feel like a discarded puppy, left out on the road by myself. I am under a doctor's care, but pills can't cure my loneliness and my yearning for love.[2]

Having loved ones nearby can ease problems of solitary living. But the worst kind of senior loneliness comes not from involuntary bereavement, but is due to voluntary withdrawal, i.e. the self-inflicted variety.

Have we overemphasized seniors' craving company? British sociologist Alex Comfort thought senior loneliness is exaggerated. They are not lonely so much as ill, he said.[3] He could have cited limited retirement incomes as a motive for closer relations among seniors. Few can afford the high cost of independent living. Two can room together almost as cheaply as one. But Alex Comfort also underestimated some retirees' desire to disengage. Many seniors prefer secured privacy. Others can become obsessively reclusive. Two examples received wide publicity:

> Howard Hughes [1905-1976], with a net worth of 2.3 billion dollars at his death, sought and secured absolute privacy after 1958. Apparently he was driven to seclusion by extreme obsessive-compulsive motives.[4]

> J. Paul Getty [1893-1975] barricaded himself in a mansion protected by fierce dogs and numerous security personnel. His few friends described him as "the loneliest man in the world."[5]

Few Americans enjoy the luxuries of those two men. Yet more are happier and less imprisoned by fears.

Retirees want intimacy. Many get only isolation. The rural poor are especially disadvantaged; their closest neighbors can be miles away. Many rural seniors have little opportunity for socializing. Urban seniors may stick to themselves out of fears that seem to increase with age. As Meals on Wheels volunteers often discover, some seniors don't leave their rooms for weeks or travel from their blocks for months. They tip willing neighbors to run their food errands. Sadder still, their children don't call or regularly visit them. Some get only yearly visits from their families.

Dr. James J. Lynch of John Hopkins University maintains that those who live alone have premature death rates two to ten times higher than those who live with others.[6] Loneliness can kill. Loneliness is not life as it should be. Seniors find camaraderie and companionship among those of their own age and interests. That helps explain why retirement villages pepper warmer climate states such as Florida and Arizona. Group housing (i.e., by age) is sometimes condemned as "age apartheid." Others see it as expression of the homogeneous unit principle. Dr. James Birren of California's USC said, "The older you get the more you want to live with people like yourself. You want, to put it bluntly, to die with your own."[7]

IS TOGETHERNESS ALWAYS DESIRABLE?

Economic and health reasons may pressure us to relocate with our adult children. But proximity can be problematic. Too much togetherness—especially under involuntary circumstances—can become maddening. Unable to afford independent living, elder parents find living with their children's families wears them out.

Cramped quarters and lost freedom can generate friction. Fatigue sets in, often accompanied by resentment. Stress increases in our children's marriage. Everyone feels uncomfortable about it all.

In nursing homes similar tensions can develop. Neglect of residents by an unsympathetic staff in exploitative institutions makes seniors' experience unbearable. Emotional, uncaring isolation from staff makes crowded conditions feel worse. While loneliness is rarely desirable, such circumstances can commend retreating solitude.

VARIETIES OF LONELINESS

To live in solitude is not necessarily to live alone. This is a vital and valuable distinction. One can be alone but not lonely.

[1] *Self-imposed vs. enforced loneliness*

All of us desire our own space, i.e. privacy. Solitude need not be isolation. The 1952 Nobel Prize winner for literature, Francois Mauriac (1885-1970) noted that for the Christian, there is "no solitude in which [God] does not join us."[8]

During periods of withdrawal—even exile from society—we can never completely withdraw from God, for He surrounds us even in our solitude. So many great changes in history have been created from times of withdrawal or exile. For the Christian, God can produce wonderful blessing from solitude. In our quiet moment we can advance God's causes and people through strong prayers.

[2] *Short-term vs. long-term loneliness*

Bank customers held hostage know *acute* loneliness, shut off from those dear to them. In the 1980s Terry Anderson, held hostage in Beirut by terrorists who allowed him only minimal privacy, experienced *chronic* loneliness because he could not return to his job, family, and nation for seven years. The widowed or unmarried, whether by choice or by providence, can live alone for many years. Long-term loneliness can turn into *chronic* loneliness. But short-term loneliness—though it may be acute—does not last.

[3] *Physical vs. spiritual loneliness*

One can be physically isolated from friends and family but continue in close and intimate fellowship with the Lord. By contrast, a drug pusher may circulate, elbow to elbow, through a jammed audience at a rock concert, yet be separated from his only Creator and Savior.

[4] *Occupational vs. personal loneliness*

A soldier or sailor "on watch" endures long hours alone. His or her vigilance allows others to sleep in safety. But sentry duty time is over at dawn, and life with others picks up again. President Lyndon Johnson referred to the White House as "lonely acres," because the responsibilities of the Presidency could be borne only by one man. Whether president of our nation or teacher of a Sunday School class, one can feel alone on the job.

Longevity itself can involve loneliness. Death of a lifelong spouse can induce severe loneliness. Funerals often turn solitude into loneliness. After the death of Prince Albert, Queen Victoria lamented, "There is no one left to call me 'Victoria.'" Death of a loved one may turn absence into anguish.

ABSORBED IN LONELINESS

Loneliness is often worse than creaky bones. It is bad enough when knees click, hips hurt, elbows lock, necks

ache, and fingers swell. But when we are leveled by
loneliness, suffering sinks to a new level. Our well-
being atrophies in loneliness. This intensifies if there is
no stimulation from loved ones. So we turn elsewhere
for companionship.

> Thou has taken all my friends from me, and made me
> loathsome to them....Thou hast taken lover and friend
> far from me, and parted me from my companions. [Ps.
> 88:8,18, NEB]

The death of a spouse is a traumatic loss. At your
wedding, God bonded the two of you to a new creation,
a One New Person. With his or her death, we feel less
than half that Person. Surviving the death of a beloved
husband or wife is far more wrenching than winding
down one's career. The double stress from losing both a
mate and a vocation compounds suffering and the pain
of loneliness.

Retirement usually puts us on a slower track. But
after we have begun fulfilling dreams of what we "have
always wanted to do," time can begin to drag. For a time
we enjoy the absence of our old work routines. But then
empty days become harder to fill. Idleness can be numb-
ing if not killing. Many without a workplace setting feel
isolated, nonproductive, listless, unsatisfied. This transition to less demanding schedules and fewer activities
may grate. Activity shifts, though voluntary, eventually
may breed disappointment, and expanded social activities aren't always its cure. If regrets dominate, resentments may build, turning us bitter.

One source of frustration for seniors is that, though
they have more free time, most have less money. Within
available means, use every opportunity to attempt new
ventures, develop latent talents, or utilize old talents in
new ways. Instead of letting yourself be pickled in your
own barrel, pray for the strength to participate!

Sickness forces us to rest. Paradoxically, rest both aids recovery and can aggravate loneliness. Another paradox appears when one shares a hospital room with another patient. We know we're not the only ones with pain and a medical problem. (In a strange way, hospitalization has the potential for cheering us up!) The sick don't want to walk on water, just to walk across the room on their own. But activities stall in a sick room; isolation can hit the immobilized. Confinement can lead to depression, and depression deprives us of incentive, interest, and optimism. That, in turn, delays recovery and may hasten organic deterioration.

THE SPIRITUAL DIMENSION OF LONELINESS

When adults purposefully or unwittingly avoid Christ by involvement with self-projects, it looks deceptively freeing. But we are meant to fellowship with Him. Anytime the Lord is unwelcome in our corner, solitude generates a spiritual vacuum.

We grow in solitude when it includes fellowship with Christ. So, solitude should not be used to fortify us against Him. Time alone with God strengthens us to return to our duties and situation renewed, refreshed, and ready to serve with new effectiveness.

When we are absolutely alone, there is no place to hide. We are vulnerable; we feel exposed. And that can open us to God's scrutiny. We have too much guilt to ignore. Being left alone we are "out there" without illusions, pretensions, and moral padding to make us look "great." But when we are alone, God can also be present to inspire our lives with the light of His Word.

Richard Wagner, the composer, couldn't accept getting old. His denial showed itself in angry outbursts against his wife.[9] Beneath his rage was self-pity. Tears often mask anger. Rage can hide denial. Demands can be a camouflage for self-pity. "Self-care" can disguise self-pity. Resentment can stimulate self-pity. All too often, self-pity is rage turned inward.

> Age takes us by surprise, and its sudden coming gives us an ill-defined feeling of injustice, a feeling that finds its expression in countless examples of resistance, defiance and refusal.[10]

JESUS, OUR BEST COMPANION

Jesus was lonely in the desert. Unlike Moses, who was surrounded by tribes that usually pestered him, Jesus had no one else around to help keep his spirits "up." Mark tells us he was surrounded by animals and angels (Mark 1:13). Strangely, Jesus wasn't even concerned about providing bread for Himself. His purpose was to bring bread to those who had none (John 6:1, 22, 35, 51). Later, the darkness of Gethsemane was like light in the wilderness: In both places Jesus sought solitude. But in both places, Satan sought Him out. All too often when we go on retreat, Satan tries to assault our spiritual vitality even in that place of meditation and dedication.

The first temptation was an appeal to lure Jesus into self-pity. "Why," Satan suggests, "why should you needlessly starve when power is at your disposal to make bread." Self-pity's allure was also strong in the second temptation. Whereas desire for self-preservation focused the first temptation, the second appealed to Jesus' possible need for protection by angels.

During the first temptation, Jesus declared the basic truth that no one, no matter how successful or self-sufficient, can bear to live apart from God. "Man cannot live on bread alone!" (Matt. 4:4). Like Job, Jesus "treasured the words of [God's] mouth more than my daily bread" (Job 23:12b, NIV). It was the sustaining power of Scripture, combined with commitment to His Father, that led Jesus to self-abdication rather than self-pity. His experience and example still inspire the lonely to gain a sense of God's care and acceptance. But He also understood lepers and the blind. He understood the aching void in those socially scorned and snubbed.

LONELINESS AS A TOLERABLE STATE

> Two are better than one, because they have a good return for their work. If one falls down, his friend can help him up! Ecclesiastes 4:9, 10 (NIV).

The telephone is a marvelous instrument for visiting with someone when physical presence is inconvenient or impossible. The telephone can be like an extended hand. "Reach out and touch someone"—a phone company slogan—captures the spirit of Ecclesiastes 4:10. We can use the phone to check on our friends, to listen to their hurt, to minister with the balm of Gilead, to pray with them though separated from them, to learn of their joys and to share in their dreams. By lifting the receiver, we may be lifting someone else's load or sharing its weight and in the process rediscover what a helping hand is all about. Alex Comfort was right. The phone "is the most important single technological resource of later years. If you can reach a telephone, you aren't alone."[11] Today, new acquaintances are made on the internet and on-line computer services. A network of friends can become an answer to prayer.

Among the best features of Christian retirement communities are the programs that engage residents in meaningful activity. Christian retirement centers may not have the funding necessary to put them on the level of some posh secular facilities. But they have something more precious and more important than plush carpets, lush lobbies, and manicured grounds. They offer residents useful spiritual programs. Most have regular Bible studies, prayer circles, and church services. And their sewing, cooking, or quilting activities are usually directed toward Christian missions.

One of the great ministries in retirement homes are resident Bible studies. Margaret, the eighty-five-year-old widow of the late Dr. Donald Grey Barnhouse, found a full life in Waverly Heights Retirement Community, near Philadelphia. She rides an electric cart. But her real satisfaction is conducting Bible studies where she can share her knowledge of Scripture.[12]

We, too, can find involvement in such exercises that help meet our spiritual needs. Indeed, sometimes they can give us a heavenly rush. The encouragement from God's Word on a sustained basis does wonders in enabling us to cope with problems and pains. By praying together and discussing the Bible, Christian retirees can find continual uplift and encouragement.

> Since I must fight if I would reign,
> Increase my courage, Lord;
> I'll bear the toil, endure the pain,
> Supported by Thy Word.

Pouting over being left by others is a trifle compared to leaving the Lord who longs for our love. Fellowship with God can defuse loneliness. Our sense of God's presence with us is a vital weapon to banish loneliness. One of the most important ways we experience God's presence leads through the doorway of personal prayer.

> …If in the joy of heaven we live,
> or only on what earth can give,
> Though pure and high—so we may learn
> Unto the soul's great good to turn.
> What thing soever best engage
> Our thoughts toward our pilgrimage,
> Which teach us this is not our rest,
> That here we are but as a guest;
> As doubtless 'twas no other thought,

That in his holy bosom wrought,...
Pleased if we feel that God is nigh,
Both where we live and where we die,
Whether among true kindred thrown,
Or seeming outwardly alone—
That, whether this or that befall,
He watches and He cares for all.[13]

WINNING WAYS

• Exchange your crying towel for a polishing cloth. Time to shine, not to whine.

• Help promote Christian programs with others in whatever setting and occasion is possible.

• Take on new responsibilities in church and community. Sign up rather than sign out.

• Use times of privacy and solitude to get your spiritual flywheel up to maximum revolutions so that you'll have the inner energy to propel you forward in God's work on earth.

THINGS TO THINK ABOUT:

[1] Loneliness has many faces. What face do you see it in? How do you view loneliness? What is your perspective on it? How would you distinguish between isolation of spirit and isolation of space?

[2] What kind of loneliness did Jesus experience in the desert?

[3] What kind of loneliness did Jesus experience in preaching? What kind of loneliness did Jesus experience in His passion and death?

[4] What kind of loneliness drains? What kind of loneliness fires us up?

[5] How is God's presence known in our lives? Read 1 Corinthians 3:16. What role does the Holy Spirit play in dispelling loneliness for Christians? How is the Holy Spirit present with us? Must we always feel He is present for Him to actually be present with us?

[6] How is God able to use our reluctance to be solitary in bridging distances between people? What kind of friendships can we develop? What relationships bring the greatest satisfaction?

12

TEMPTED TO
WORRY

Fear not, I am with thee,
Oh be not dismayed:
For I am thy God, and will still give thee aid;
I'll strengthen thee, help thee,
And cause thee to stand
Upheld by my righteous omnipotent hand,
Upheld by my righteous omnipotent hand.[1]
—George Keith [1639-1716]

Worry affects everyone. A kindergarten child worries when she is dropped off at school for the first time. Mothers worry how the child is adjusting. Teenagers feel anxious about looking dumpy or dorky. A new father worries that company re-engineering may eliminate his job.

Fears and worry are often found together because they feed upon each other. They coexist in us and can be dynamically linked. Yet they do have distinct identities. They are different and give us trouble in different ways, at different levels and times.

Because we confuse fear with worry, they become difficult to overcome. By understanding how they function, we can be in a better position to cope with them. And to do that, we must know how they operate.

When fearful, we expect the worst. Fear is a pervasive apprehension about an unpleasant outcome. Worry is a pervasive uncertainty about a good outcome. Fear can incapacitate us and cause adverse physical reactions.

A "house bound" impulse is fear of open places, the impulse which makes one avoid contact with the public. Anyone who refuses to go out is afraid of gathered people. It is called agoraphobia.

Anxiety, however, differs from fear: [1] First, because while persistent it is a diffused attitude of uneasiness rather than a conscious, specific dread, and [2] anxiety differs from fear by the absence of certainty. "True anxiety is being afraid but having no idea what it is that you fear."[2]

An anxious person is racked by uncertainty. A worrier feels unsafe. Whereas the phobic person has a negative certainty and expects specific harm, the anxious person experiences pervasive uncertainty about any outcomes.

Is All Anxiety Sinful?

All fears are not evil. For example, there is the fear of the Lord—even in His presence—without dread (Prov. 10:27; 19:23). But what about anxiety? Is all anxiety sinful?

Scriptural injunctions "not to worry" concern God's oversight and control of life. In Matthew 6:25-34 Jesus referred to worry six times and in each instance the point was that we should avoid being overly anxious about having our needs met. We should plan ahead prudently. Plans should be undergirded with trust that God wants the best for us. Anxiety doesn't add to our longevity; it shortens life spans. "Cast your cares on the

Lord and he will sustain you" (Ps. 55:22, NIV; 1 Peter 5:7).

It is not evil to care, but care becomes evil when we do not turn our concerns over to God's lordship. Paul advised the Philippians, "Do not be anxious about anything, but in everything by prayer and petition, with thanksgiving, present your requests to God" (Phil. 4:6, NIV). The first part of the verse—"do not be anxious about anything"—would seem to suggest that all anxiousness is evil.

Are there not some things we should be anxious about? Legitimate cares require attention. In the same letter Paul, himself, confessed to being deeply concerned:

> ...I am all the more eager to send [Epaphroditus], so that when you see him again you may be glad and I may have less anxiety. (Philippians 2:28, NIV)

A few verses earlier Timothy was held up as a sterling servant of Christ because he took a genuine interest in the Philippians' spiritual welfare (2:20). Paul felt concern for the churches daily (2 Cor. 11:28). Each Christian should care for his fellow believer (1 Cor. 12:25), just as one part of our body cares for the welfare of its other members. Being overly concerned turns into sinful anxiety when we fail to seek the Lord's presence in that concern.

Apply this principle elsewhere. If Scripture condemned all anxiety, it would be sinful to feel anxious about learning a subject, mastering a trade, or embarking on a major new venture. Small doses of anxiety drive us to master a subject, hone a skill, perfect a performance, and prepare us for an impending danger so we can act prudently. In small amounts, fear and anxiety contribute to our health, to our success, and to Christian growth.

We're talking about amounts. The right dosage of the drug Belladonna, for instance, helps settle upset stomachs, but a large intake kills. As in prescription drugs, so in the Christian life: A little anxiety pushes life forward; a large amount of anxiety maims, slows, and destroys life.

A smidgen of anxiety is constructive and can stimulate a person toward excellence. For instance, a mild amount of uncertainty will motivate a Sunday School teacher to study faithfully during the week rather than wait until late Saturday night to prepare. Prolonged, intense anxiety, however, can emotionally cripple us. Because of it, we lose confidence, perhaps even temporary memory loss in the midst of teaching.

What needs to be done first is to neutralize false guilt about anxiety. Be discerning. Christian seniors should exercise hardheaded self-scrutiny about feelings and fears. Distinguish between anxieties given over to God and those that cripple active faith.

In early Methodism, its leaders appealed to sinners to come to the "anxious bench," a front seat where sincere inquiry was made about receiving of divine pardon. Later, nineteenth-century evangelist Charles Grandison Finney [1792-1875] mentioned the "anxious meeting," the "anxious room," and the "anxious seat."[3] Any Christian who lacked the assurance of salvation was anxious about his or her eternal destiny. Prayers before an evangelistic event were for God to bring sinners out of their apathy into a proper concern, a healthy anxiety about their relationship with God.

If all concerns were evil, then why would God be involved in creating spiritual anxiety? The Holy Spirit comforts the grieving and makes the spiritually smug uncomfortable. Some self-doubt is the result of the convicting presence of God's Spirit. Our uncertainty about our distance from Christ or our shallow relationship with Him should agitate desire to know Him better and to love Him more. If God did not use anxiety about our eternal destiny, we would feel no compulsion to seek the Lord. God also uses anxiety to stimulate us into Christian maturity.

Some anxieties are of God; others are of the Devil. Sorting out which anxieties are divinely generated and which ones are satanically injected is no simple task. It requires knowledge of the Bible far beyond a superficial acquaintance. Scripture ministers to our emotions. It involves transposing daily Bible reading to a new level of personal application. We must learn to size up our feelings critically.

Is All Fear Sinful?

A healthy fear can save a life. For instance, anticipate the foolishness of heating several rooms by leaving the kitchen stove on. It may cause a house fire. An improperly vented portable kerosene heater can asphyxiate. A healthy fear and common sense tells us we'd better have it properly vented. A furnace heat exchanger, if cracked, will leak deadly carbon dioxide. Get a new furnace; keep your life.

Is our fear of the dark a regression to childlike fears? Or are we reacting to the fact that crimes are often committed under the cover of darkness? After all, darkness itself is not always our concern; it is what the dark may conceal or encourage.

Failing eyesight explains why many seniors don't go out at night. But why do those with good eyesight also avoid night travel? Irrational worries regarding daylight activities halt numerous ventures. How silly to worry about things that pose little or no threat to us.

Too many waste time brooding about disappointments and dangers. Apprehensions can shorten our lives. Type A seniors are just as inclined as their younger counterparts to be unable to relax. Although retirement can mean fewer duties and deadlines, new anxieties may emerge.

Do you have health fears? Are you worried about acceptance by others? Beware. Lowered self-esteem can simmer for a long time before flaming up in such forms. Self-reproach often is a form of anxiety hiding unresolved hostilities that may go way back.

Jonathan Swift [1667-1745] was known for his acerbic wit, his bilious pessimism, as well as for his fertile imagination. He felt himself unjustly criticized and persecuted. In later life he swerved into a pattern of self-vindication which had all the appearance of self-dislike. He was consumed by resentment. Unstable, fretful, and tormented by gout, he imagined enemies and saw only the dark side of life. His disdain for others was a reflection of his own self-distrust. "When his friends celebrated his seventieth birthday, he said bitterly, 'I am no more than a shadow of myself.'"[4]

Anxiety attracts, reflects, and reinforces bad attitudes toward others. Why do anxiety attacks reflect such attitudes? Counseling cases reveal that we often project on others our own guilt feelings. When we berate others, sometimes we're unhappy with our own behaviors. Suspicion of others can arise from self-doubt or anger about our own frustrations and failure to find fulfillment. Many anxieties spring from and feed ego imbalance.

DOES ANXIETY TAPER OFF WITH AGE?

A lifetime of contented living leaves many of us not self-satisfied but sure-footed. If we seem blasé about problems, it is not because our nerves are shattered, but we have learned to commit cares to Him who cares for us.

Financial security should lessen our anxieties. But most people work hard, maintain their health, excel in their vocations to remain financially solvent, and consequently are neither lassoed by excessive worries nor boxed in by fears. Thankfully, many seniors can shake off worry.

Some centenarians, however, remain physically tough though consumed by worry. Becky Thomas, a 106-year-old Altoona, Pennsylvania woman, was featured by UPI. She could not stop worrying about her eighty-year-old daughter, who has the same name. According to the octogenarian, her daughter "puts things down and can't remember where she's put them. When I put things some place I know where they are. She gets along worse than I do."[5]

Like resilient dandelions, fears have deep roots. You think you've gotten rid of them but they come back. That also happens with anxiety. Old anxieties often take on a demonic energy. As in the parable of the cleansed house, after the house is swept clean they return with an even nastier character. Symptoms of anxiety swoop back upon us like an "obedient" Australian boomerang from another angle. Fears can pack wallop comparable to a spring trap. Let's be realistic, fellow Christian: we may reduce our anxieties, but we should never expect to be totally delivered from them.

WHAT IS YOUR ANXIETY TOLERANCE LEVEL?

Godly dissatisfaction with our situation stimulates us to improve. But when anxiety turns into an obsession, bizarre behavior usually follows.

Return to the sad example of Howard Hughes. He had a lot of business credits to his name and amassed a large fortune over his lifetime, but he died looking like a wild man. Mixed into his hygienic panic was the pollution of vanity. As a pilot he sustained three air crashes. Those crashes left him with some facial disfigurement (broken nose and cheeks). Such disfigurement drove him deeper into social withdrawal. He stayed away from the public, too, out of fear of contamination or fear that others might gain power over him. Indeed, he became tyrannical in dealing with his closest staff. Hughes' health quirks may have begun with a God-given self-protection feeling ("no man hates his own flesh") but they grew into an abnormal obsession. What started off as a valid desire to preserve and protect his life ended with compulsive reclusive behavior.[6]

Seniors should not let legitimate health concerns develop into delusory fears and destructive anxieties. It is one thing to be cautious. It is another to be so insulated by fear that normal relations are curtailed. The habituation of avoidance allows diffused anxieties to become a pretext for social hibernation. Don't let any anxiety get so out of hand that it cuts off our contact with others.

WHAT WORRIES SENIORS?

The Old Testament poem on aging, Ecclesiastes 12, put adult fears within the larger context of the aging process.[7] Five fears were mentioned in that passage.

[1] *Heights*

Old age was described as a time "when men are afraid of heights" (Ecclesiastes 12:5 NIV).

In Xenia, Ohio, there is a company (Skydive: Green County Bungee Jumping) that promises to fit customers with a full-body harness or an ankle harness and let you jump and bounce from a 150-foot crane—all for just $65. By 1992, steps were taken to have the apparatus pass state safety requirements so it could be featured at the Ohio State Fair. Dan Stone, a partner in the Xenia company, says the sport is "spreading like wild fire."[8] Bungee jumping may give a "rush" (of adrenaline), but for some readers the only rush would be to the hospital! For me and, possibly for you, to become a human yo-yo is no temptation.

A hundred-year-old man, S. L. Potter of Alpine, California, however, defied age, common sense, the pleas of his daughters (who ranged from age sixty-eight to seventy-four), and the advice of his physician to shun a dare to bungee jump from a 210-foot tower. He wanted to get in the *Guinness Book of World Records* as the world's oldest bungee jumper. His dear ones feared he would die trying it. Before he jumped, he admitted it could be fatal. Yet, he said, "If I die, I die. I told everybody to bring a shovel and a mop just in case."[9]

[2] *Housing*

Ironically, property in which seniors seek security against anxiety can become the locus for new anxieties. Repair bills increase, upkeep is an unwelcome chore, and the fear of being taken advantage of by unscrupulous contractors is a real worry.

Going from the old homestead to a retirement center has its own built-in potential for anxiety. Retirees may first wonder—then worry—about losing their liberty moving into facilities that have rules and regulations. They'd prefer to be self-sustaining and self-directed. The decision to enter a well-managed elder-care facility is not easy and not without pain. Many eventually must take this step.

Trust in the Lord can go a long way to sustain us in the transition: "Fear not to go down into Egypt," said God to Jacob (Gen. 46:3). Moses faced similar anxiety over leaving Egypt. God said to him, "I will go with you in person and set your mind at rest" (Ex. 33:14, NEB). God would have the same encouragements apply to overly anxious elders who face relocation and adjustment. New quarters require new relationships. Although our dignity, morale, and sense of continued usefulness are part of self-maintenance, it is also true that God can use a new, smaller environment to provide occasions to trust Him, new opportunities to experience His peace, and a new place to witness to His grace.

Moving into smaller quarters also means getting rid of things. That is part of the heartache. Separating from prized possessions can be agonizing. But there can be valuable trade-offs. If this prospect faces us, being light-hearted about it can make our responsibility list shrink. It just means we have fewer things to worry about.

Part of the growth challenge is intergenerational contact. That, too, is important for seniors to maintain good mental health. The benefits are many. In cases where adult children welcome parents to move in with them, primary responsibilities of meal preparation often pass on to the adult son or daughter. Under these circumstances, chances are good that elderly parents will eat better and enjoy healthier meals. In addition to keeping grandparents more youthful, an added advantage is that seniors will be in a setting more oriented toward the future and stuck less in the past.

[3] *Money and Health Worries*

Finances can be a worry to retirees. Fixed retirement income is often meager. Although widows are the largest group of shareholders in US corporations, there are still plenty of destitute widows. Widows on fixed income with little or no pension or savings find it hard to meet bills. While churches may step in to supplement their needy through deacons' Good Samaritan or similar designated funds, some seniors also face having their low-rent apartment being torn down for city expansion or for real state development. Then, on top of that, there's creeping inflation and unforeseen medical costs not covered by Medicare. Savings can evaporate overnight. Prolonged medical care can quickly drain life savings. Pressured in their pocketbook, seniors ask, "Can God spread a table in [my] desert?" (Ps. 78:19).

Realize that God has included us in His divine protection program. In our sufferings God supplies strength to live with and work through our problems. The Lord sometimes seems to provide too sparingly, but there is always enough strength available to keep us going. Paul counted on the Lord's intervention in his dire circumstances even as he counseled struggling Philippians to look to His love as a bottomless bounty. "And my God will meet all your needs according to his glorious riches in Christ Jesus.' (Phil. 4;19, NIV).

[4] *Life's Length and Death's Approach*

Thanatophobia is the fear of death. Psychologist Carl Jung said that he had yet to meet a patient over age forty whose problems were not somehow tied to his or her fear of death. The ultimate anxiety for all persons, however, should be about what lies beyond their death. No matter how much cause for pessimism in life faces us, Christians have marvelous optimism about death's aftermaths. Eternal life in Christ redeems earthly disappointments. I've provided more comment on the Christian's future life in *Probing Heaven*, a major work on heaven, still available.[10]

[5] *Worries in Living Alone*

Widowhood can compound sorrow. Loneliness follows that loss. Two famous Bible widows, Naomi and Anna, can revitalize us in our circumstances. See my book *Too Young To Be Old*.[11] Our Lord pictured a widow deprived of help beseeching a judge for justice. The lesson drawn from that portrait was for all widowed to not only to pray but pester—yes, to even pester God (Luke 18:1-8).

THREE WAYS TO CHALLENGE
AND CHANNEL WORRIES

[1] *Sort them out*

First, size down anxieties by recognizing substantial differences in them. Anxiety or worry can either be transitory or a continuing personality trait. Some people worry only about specific matters; others are troubled about everything. Dread is rampant worry. But emergencies may produce acute anxiety attacks. Thankfully, emergencies usually pass. Instead of waiting for worry to attack them, seniors can attack worry.

a. *Attack acute anxiety.* Unaddressed fears or unresolved anxieties produce multiple fears. The best way to bring a swift end to acute anxiety is to tackle a pressing problem immediately rather than just hope it will go away. When addressed decisively and intentionally, apprehension diminishes. Then there is one less thing to go bump in the night or kerplunk in the day.

b. *Chronic anxiety* refers to persistent worry. It means the person is unsure about all aspects of life. *Chronic worry* is not temporary but verges on addiction, a chronic response toward whatever comes along. Unimportant events get inflated all of out of proportion because there is no Big Picture for distinguishing them from more important matters. Knowing that God works all things for Christians' good (Rom. 8:28) means believers are not victims of haphazard luck or purposeless flukes. God's purposes will prevail. This is our Father's world. Knowing that He is in control of all things should dash the chronic worry that we are victims of chance and diminish any fussiness that would deny the complete fulfillment of His will. We can begin to overcome chronic worry, first by stopping our whining. God's sovereign involvement in His world means our lives are special to Him.

[2] *Work them out*

Moderate physical activity does wonders in relieving tension and stress. It improves our muscle tone, breathing, burns off extra weight, and gives greater stamina. Participation in regular physical activity will not prevent aging, but it will keep our circulatory system and vital organs in better shape.

Sit-down activities, such as making pot holders or quilting also uses energy while giving satisfaction. In addition to helping others, we help ourselves.

Seniors like and benefit from routines. Habit is a subtle form of letting more tranquil features of our past be perpetuated. Simone de Beauvoir said that seniors' old habits "protect [them from] generalized anxieties by assuring [them] that tomorrow will be a repetition of today."[12] Routines also spare us from having to adapt to unnecessary changes.

[3] *Pray them out*

Prayer can become our chief means to control, reduce, and expel needless worries—especially when it matures beyond just repeating favorite prayers. Prayer also is a time for listening to our Lord. Frequent prayer also builds a hedge against a worry's reoccurrence, especially when it helps us discern the difference between wants and real needs. The book of Psalms is a marvelous manual showing how others spoke with their Lord about needs—including the need to praise God and count their real blessings. Reading a daily psalm can provide us with inspiration and example for effective prayer.

Every anxious moment is a call to prayer. John Calvin said: "it is by much anxiety that the fervor of prayer is inflamed"[13] "Let every faithful heart pray to You in the hour of anxiety; when great floods threaten...When anxious thoughts fill my heart, your comfort brought me joy." (Pss. 32:6; 94:19, REB). In distress, David praised and prayed. The day of trouble was his opportunity to trust God (Ps. 18:6). Isaiah said, "I will trust and not be afraid" (12:2). Divine care and assurance are especially conveyed to us through the window of prayer.

Jesus said, Consider the ravens; they do not sow or reap, they have no storeroom or barn; yet God feeds them. And how much more valuable you are than birds! (Luke 12:24, NIV)

Jesus reminds us, that worry reflects badly on God's caring. As the lowliest birds aren't abandoned by God, neither are we.

> Said the robin to the sparrow,
> "I should really like to know
> Why these anxious human brings
> Rush about and worry so."
> Said the sparrow to the robin:
> "Friend, I think that it must be
> That they have no heavenly Father,
> Such as cares for you and me."[14]
> —Elizabeth Cheney

J. C. Penny Found Wealth in the Lord

In 1931 at age fifty-six, J. C. Penny was a broken man in a Battle Creek, Michigan sanitarium. Mr. Penny, who opened his first store in Kemmerer, Wyoming, lost his fortune during the Great Depression. In a sanitarium corridor, he heard the strains of the familiar hymn, "God Will Take Care of You."

> Be not dismayed whatever betide,
> God will take care of you....

Then he heard Matthew 11:28 read over the loudspeaker: "Come unto me, all ye that labor and are heavy laden, and I will give you rest." Penny said, "A weight lifted from my spirit. I came out a different man, renewed."[15]

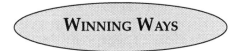

WINNING WAYS

• Our badge of Christian confidence is a beaming face.

• Share with others your thanksgiving for God's goodness through the years.

• As the apostle James suggested, hedge your plans with the still-useful phrase, "If the Lord wills...."

• Bask in the sunlight of God's love rather than retreat into the shadowy caves of human despair.

Things to Think About:

[1] How do anxieties about life during our younger years compare to anxieties about life nearer its end?

[2] List your most frequent fears. How did they originate? How were they formed? How have they changed or grown when combined with other fears? Next, compare them with specific blessings in your life.

[3] What kinds of fears or anxieties now bother us?

[4] Can we see God's hand and purposes leading us to a deeper, true understanding of ourselves and of Himself in our unique histories?

[5] How else can we deal with our fears and anxieties so that we grow in Christ all the more—through them?

13

TEMPTED TO
DESPAIR

An Austin, Texas nursing home survey revealed "persons in the non-institutional sample who read the Bible once a week or oftener were more likely to have a high level of adjustment that those who reported reading the Bible less often."[1]
—Richard M. Gray and David O. Moberg

Early retirement can delight like a surprise rainbow after a sudden summer shower. Across retirement's rainbow lies a spectrum of colorful days. Usually it is a fantastic blessing, freeing one to enjoy life while opening up opportunities to serve God in new ways.

But some seniors discover at the end of their rainbow not a pot of gold, but a pond of dreary days and long nights. After the initial exhilaration and freshness of being one's own boss wears off and new routines turn dull, chances are good that old sadnesses, loneliness, and depression pound us and erode our beach of dreams.

Some try to liquidate their depression in slow afternoons and long nights by drinking alcoholic beverages. It has long been known that depression is a leading cause of habitual drinking. Older adults can be highly susceptible to depression and its by-product, excessive drinking.

Depression often increases with age. Not only is it a common affective disorder, but significant numbers of seniors have a propensity to it. This is not an unfair stereotyping, nor does it create a pseudo senior *persona*. Case studies show the most common psychiatric disorder among seniors is depression.[2] Because the percentage of diagnosed depression ranges from thirty to sixty-five percent in those over sixty, it means a sizable and growing segment of American seniors battle this problem.[3]

Depression is a temptation because it can develop as a seemingly logical alternative to losses, problems, and loneliness. It is also a temptation on a secondary level: depression can follow times of high stress. Of all the temptations that plague older adults, depression (and its companion—despair) do most to push us to the point of giving up.

DEPRESSION: MEDICAL AND MENTAL

Shallow moralists do a gross injustice when they label all depression as simple attitudinal failure to adjust. Yes, depression can belong on the modern list of deadly sins, but it is equally connected with complex and intricate body chemistry. Physicians distinguish between varieties of depression.

Seasonal/Situational Depression

No one ever fully escapes occasional disappointment, letdown, and loss. The death of a loved one is an inescapable agony. Grief is hard to overcome. Then, there's the weather and how it can affect our attitude. Studies show that sustained cold, such as is encountered by polar expeditions, makes people irritable. People feel down during a deep-freeze. Rainy days can have a similar effect.

But sometimes reactive, affective disorders go deeper than circumstances and have psychological roots.

Clinical/Chemical Depression

The late Sir Winston Churchill suffered from spells of depression all through life,[4] but nothing on the order of former astronaut "Buzz" Aldrin. Aldrin had been to the moon and back. After his moon mission, he was struck down with extreme mental depression that required hospitalization.[5]

The bipolar disorder of manic-depression is characterized by cycles of mania, depression, and stable behavior. Psychotic behavior may accompany mania. But not always. The mania cycle includes an irritated and elevated mood, excessive emotional outbursts, grandiose thoughts, raving thought and rapid talk. The depression cycle includes troubled concentration, suicidal thoughts, and low self-esteem. One common drug treatment is lithium (see the Appendix ["Psychopharmacology and Depression"] for more information on drugs and depression). Clinical depression requiring hospitalization and medication may begin with an acute onslaught, totally immobilizing the patient. This type of depression is organically based, resulting from biological and chemical changes in the brain and endocrine system.[6]

Our psychological well-being and body chemistry are intricately interconnected. The limbic system (in the brain), hormone imbalance (carried by the blood stream) and the adrenal gland affect the rise and fall of depression. Its biochemical aspects do not mean, however, that depression is solely physical. Some clinical depressions make a belated, late-life appearance. After age sixty, for instance, thyroid disease and vitamin deficiency can trigger deep depressions. To what degree and at what level our moral values affect or are affected by body/ brain malfunctioning has never been finally and fully determined.

Hereditary Factors in Depression

The characters of Winnie the Pooh include Eeyore the donkey. Eeyore expected the worst from everyone. He represents the pessimist in any age. If someone says to an Eeyore-type individual that he was a "quality person," that person would take it as meaning he was of poor quality. Anyone genetically predisposed to depression should beware of being influenced by negative Eeyore characters. There is some agreement, however, that functional depression connects with organic abnormalities and hereditary predispositions. Some clinical evidence points to chromosomal influence in manic-depressive illnesses.[7]

Constitutional predisposition to depression appears in some notably talented individuals. English novelist Charlotte Bronte [1816-1855] had a notoriously depressing temperament. Her chief biographer, Elizabeth Gaskell, guessed that Charlotte's down disposition "must have been, so to speak, constitutional, or, perhaps, from the deep pang of losing her two elder sisters combined with a permanent state of bodily weakness in producing her hopelessness."[8]

Depression patterns occasionally emerge in childhood. Hyperkinetic children often experience severe depression. For them, genetic predisposition combines with functional trauma. Together with chromosomal factors, the loss or absence of a mother contributes to their despair.[9] Childhood losses often carry over into their adult life, including senior years.

How Do We Recognize Depression?

Immediate despair in seniors can result from a number of bodily changes:

—hair loss and/or graying

—hearing and sight impairment

—reduction of kidney function with diminishing bladder control and capacity

—dwindling of hormone output, including sexual drive

—wrinkling and skin drying

—shrinking muscles, joint stiffness and swelling

—reduction of pumped blood and lung intake of oxygen

Depression among seniors frequently accompanies changing one's residence. Compulsory late-life residence change may contribute to despair. New surroundings can be bewildering and generate bitterness. Unable to continue a former lifestyle, one can experience powerlessness. And despair can set in when the arrangement's finality sinks in.

Perhaps the deepest despair, however, arises from total dependency. Total dependency refers to the need for assistance in feeding, clothing, and toilet needs. Assistance in these areas is a mercy but also an indignity. An eighty-four-year-old nursing home resident, Anna Mae Halgrim Seaver, wrote of her embarrassment and humiliation in wearing a diaper.[10]

In Tim Stafford's "Week of Days," dependency appears on Day/Five. The likelihood of dependency ascends on three major plateaus:

ages 65-74—3.5 percent are dependent seniors

ages 75-84—11 percent are dependent seniors

ages 85 and above—35 percent are dependent seniors[11]

Despair varies among seniors, but none of us totally escapes it. "Their worst fear in becoming a burden has come true." It could help seniors facing a dependency[12] situation to recall that God likened Israel to being carried by him from youth to old age (Isaiah 46:3,4).

Depression has various symptoms. One author listed seventeen such as withdrawal, fatigue, and self-deprecation. Many overlap. All relate to feeling low, down, listless, hopeless. But another root-stem condition of depression is anger. Anger is a negative emotion our egos have difficulty acknowledging. Suppressed anger increases its effects.

Wherever there is depression, anger usually lurks just below the surface. Depression, to put it another way, is often camouflaged anger and rage. In repressing fury, we wallow in self-pity and despair. Tears also can reveal anger. Anger can be hidden in excessively bubbly reactions, in crying, or in the silent treatment. Compulsive cheerfulness can disguise depression.[13] Depressed older adults can be driven by secret angers about the past, their aging, relationships, or their dependency on others.

How Have Christians Dealt With Depression in the Past?

Familiar Old and New Testament characters experienced depression. When Esau married a Hittite woman, it was a source of grief for his parents, Isaac and Rebekah (Gen. 26:34). Isaac's apprehensions sped ahead to Jacob, (Rebekah's favorite), and he feared hopelessness if Jacob also married a Hittite woman. He said, "My life will not be worth living!" (Gen. 27:46, NIV). Later, a blue mood hit Jacob in his old age, when he moaned about his missing sons. "Everything is against me" (Gen. 42:36, NIV). In a moment of despair, Moses called for his own execution (Num. 11:15). Job's despair was proverbial; he lamented his own birth:

> Why...did you bring me out of the womb? I wish I had died before my eye saw me. If only I had never come into being, or had been carried straight from the womb to the grave. (Job 10:18, 19, NIV)

When David was hunted, he despaired, "no one cares for my life" (Ps. 142:4). His son (Solomon) later wrote, "low spirits sap one's strength" (Prov. 17:22, REB).

Have you ever thought of the great Apostle Paul as depressed? Paul, for instance, did not refuse to verbalize his frustration, humiliation, and disappointment over the spiritually wishy-washy commitment of Galatian Christians (Gal. 4:11). Similar expressions of depression appeared in his correspondence with the church at Corinth (2 Cor. 1:8; 2:12-13). The Apostle felt great sadness concerning the unbelief of his fellow Jews (Rom. 9:2).

How did Paul reconcile his faith with foul moods? In the midst of a "bad news" litany to the Corinthians, glad tidings of God's intervention cheered him (2 Cor. 4:7-18; 6:4-16). No matter how low he felt, Paul rebounded with an indomitable spirit of contentment over God's mercies in his life—he counted his blessings!

Other notable Christians have struggled with a despair possibly greater than Paul's. Charles Haddon Spurgeon [1834-1892] had a brilliant intellect, a marvelous voice, and a successful world-wide ministry. Yet he had his darker moments. Astonishingly, this talented man, whose mind overflowed with tremendous biblical insights, occasionally despaired to the point of total exhaustion and prostration. His health began to deteriorate in 1871. Although Spurgeon basked in the sunshine of Scripture, he battled physical and psychological pressures. In the 1870s and 1880s he sought and found renewal at Hotel Beau Rivage, Mentone, France. He stayed there during the fall-winter seasons.[14] Even after he moved to his new home at Norwood (called "Westwood"), he struggled with despondency, a fact he shared with his congregation.[15]

OVERCOMING DEPRESSION/DESPAIR

A Theology of Suffering Can Ease Depression

Seniors with an overly materialistic outlook have more reasons to despair than those who put God's kingdom first. To value security—even wealth and power—over knowing and growing in Christ hollows rather than hallows our sunset years. We are not recommending that Christians should ignore realities of daily life or fail to plan ahead wisely. Not at all! Instead of either/or, "seek ye first the kingdom of God" amounts to keep life's needs in a Christ-centered perspective.

For the Christian, feeling down often does more damage than falling down. If we go into retirement expecting to see a bluebird of happiness perched on our window sill, don't be surprised if what lands there is the motley chicken of depression.

When cast down, do we worry whether our fellowship with God is phony? Do we equate inconsolable depression with failure to rely on Him? Philip Henry [1631-1696], the father of commentator Matthew Henry, seemed to identify depression about poor health as a sign of spiritual sickness. He wrote, "Old age is often attended with deafness, blindness, lameness; but to quarrel with these, is to quarrel with God. They are the fruits of sin."[16]

In bouts with physical weakness and weariness, we can rest in God's everlasting arms even as we work and pray for recovery. Transform miserable circumstances into opportunities to praise God for other blessings from times past, many of which continue. God works when we pray—including to enlighten us as to what our real needs are. Prayer also helps release endorphins and other positive body energies into our system, contributing to a better-regulated biochemical balance.

Confront Depression

We can address depression in all three major dimensions: the dietary, the physiological, and the spiritual. The way out of circumstantial depression, which requires neither surgical intervention or heavy medication, may be as simple as paying attention to these essentials:

[1] proper diet
[2] regular exercise
[3] injecting humor
[4] medical supervision
[5] spiritual renewal
[6] Christian fellowship.

Diet—Irregular eating habits and poor food selection indirectly contribute to feeling down. Proper eating habits help us maintain stable mental and physical health. By contrast, despondency can make us lose interest in eating nutritious meals. We hurt our physical and emotional health by substituting snacks and junk food for a good diet.

Exercise—Along with a balanced diet, regular exercise is important for physical stamina, organ function, and good mental health. Many football seasons ago retired linebacker Ray Nitschke, a dominant lineman for the Green Bay Packers, found that sitting at home watching professional football was a trial for him. He said that after watching the Packers he was so wound up that he had to jog for two miles. Jogging can "act as a tranquilizer."[17] Many people can't jog, of course. For them, brisk sustained walking is preferred. Whatever regular exercise we choose helps us to work off anxiety and prolong and enrich our lives.

Mrs. Mary Johnston, an eighty-eight-year-old grandmother from Coaltown, Oklahoma was believed to be the oldest, longest-active newspaper carrier in the nation. In thirty-four years of service, she missed only one delivery. Six times a week she delivered 164 papers. "People tell me to take it easy, but why should I? I'm as fit and healthy as I've ever been. I'd never give it up for the world."

Humor—[18] Our pain may hide a paradox. For instance, God may be sparing us from something worse. But laughter lifts. Proverbs 17:22 (NRSV) summarized the psychic/physical value of humor. "A cheerful heart is a good medicine, but a downcast spirit dries up the bones." In his *Poetics,* Aristotle wrote a profound insight: Tragedy and comedy are two sides of the same coin—the experience of Surprise. Surprises with a blessed outcome are "comedy." Those with unhappy endings are "tragedy." Our Lord is a God of blessed surprises, in Scripture and in our own lives.

Medical Supervision (Hospitalization)—If depression incapacitates us, chances are that we suffer from a biochemical imbalance which requires medical diagnosis and treatment. In many cases, depression is not a barometer of spiritual commitment but of biochemical imbalance and malfunction. Sustained, severe depression requires professional and medical attention—not guilt or spiritual doubt.

Spiritual Renewal—Attention Deficit Disorder (ADD) is sometimes associated with hyperactive youth. But the inability to concentrate or read for extended periods takes distinctive form for seniors. Short attention spans also can have a detrimental spiritual effect. Light therapy is now being used to treat some despondency disorders. During long winters, when darkness starts in the afternoon, depression is relieved for patients who spend time before massive light output lamps. Spending an hour or so reading the Bible sometimes can have a similar effect on our spirits.

Erik Erickson, an eminent Harvard psychiatrist and psycho-historian (e.g. *Young Man Luther*), said the last of life's seven phases is "not senescence but (tactfully) mature age. If we have genuinely matured, we can look back with affirmation and gratitude. But if we have failed to do more than merely endure as organisms, and thus lack a core of integrity, we find ourselves filled with disgust and despair."[19]

Isaiah referred to Israel's despair over their Babylonian captivity. They were baffled and frazzled by national disaster and personal loss. They felt dejected. It was as though their emotional wings had been clipped. By returning to the Lord, however, they could surmount desolation and long-term deprivations. Waiting on their Lord was a key to not being emotionally grounded by their circumstances (Isa. 40:30-31). "The Lord gives vigor to the weary, new strength to the exhausted" (Isa. 40:29 NEB). Those who pray with confidence in God's love and mercy are using the thermal drafts of trouble to soar over their circumstances.

> When all things seem against us,
> To drive us to despair,
> We know one gate is open,
> One ear will hear our prayer.
> —Oswald Allen

The Apostle Paul could have sunk into a murky mood every time he recalled the injustices he endured. After

cataloging his ordeals (2 Cor. 4:8-12), he concluded with
confidence:

> Therefore we do not lose heart. Though outwardly we
> are wasting away, yet inwardly we are being renewed
> day by day. For our light and momentary troubles are
> achieving for us an eternal glory that far outweighs
> them all. (vv 16-17, NIV)

Paul used the Psalms. If you are laid low, reflect on one
of the Psalms. You may see your own situation addressed there. Look at Psalms 42 and 43. The writer
probably was a Korahite priest exiled among the
Armaeans of Damascus (the "ungodly nation" of 43:1).
In a nostalgic flashback, he recalls the sylvan setting of
his former tranquil days and of the abundance of invigorating scenes from nature (42:6,7). But it was God
Himself who could only satisfy the quenching thirst of
his soul (42:1). The psalmist knew he had not measured
up. He was baffled and astonished at himself. That was
why he rebuked, cajoled, counseled, and encouraged
himself. The patient was also his own physician.

> Why are you downcast, O my soul?
> Why so disturbed within me?
> Put your hope in God,
> for I will yet praise him,
> my Savior and my God.
>   Ps. 43:5 NIV

Psalmist David could shed his gloom only to the degree
that he kept his hope fixed on the Lord. "...The Lord lifts
up those who are bowed down...." (Ps. 146:8, NIV).

Christian Fellowship—God delights when we seek Him,
one-on-One. But we should not overlook the fact that
God's presence also is given to us through our fellowship in the body of Christ. Christian friends form a

helpful network in praying for us and in encouraging us.

Of course, family circles and Christian friends cannot believe for us. We have to exercise our own prayer lungs. Yet other Christians can be supportive and remind us we are not alone in our troubles. By praying together and sharing our difficulties, we find that our coping energies increase. Christians need other Christians. Effective uplift goes beyond more institutional church involvement. Mere attachment to church roles won't help much when the church lacks the clear gospel, depriving us of Christ-centered dedication.

Paul used the harmonious interaction of the human body as an illustration of how Christian and Christian should relate and interact. (1 Cor. 12:12-31). He argued that the body's organs cannot function independently. The kidneys can't function without the heart and the lungs cannot continue without being hooked up to the kidneys. The vitality of the total body gives support to individual organs. Thus, our faith cannot battle back against despair unless we retain vital connection with the body of Christ.

In John Bunyan's *Pilgrim's Progress*, the chief character, Christian, met the hazard of the Slough of Despond. The Slough of Despond was a grizzly assortment of fears, doubts, and discouraging apprehensions. "This is the reason of the badness of this ground."

Fortunately, many Christians are not bothered by depression. Perhaps you are one with a radiant, sunny, and resilient disposition, one on whom dark clouds have no lasting effect. Some people begin life happy and never lose that outlook.

Dr. A. T. Pierson, a popular American preacher, was called to Spurgeon's pulpit in 1891 and succeeded him the following year at the Metropolitan Tabernacle. Pierson asked a young girl to give her testimony before the elders of how she came to Christ. She shocked them by saying that she had no experience to talk of. She continued: "I'm still young. I do know that Jesus said, 'Come unto Me,' and I went. He said, 'I will give you rest,' and I believe Him." One of the elders present asked, "But don't you know the Slough of Despond (discouragement), my dear?" "No, sir," she answered forthrightly, "I did not come that way!"

Depressed Christians need spiritual renewal in the worst way. In certain cases, a physician's prescription is important for regaining the proper biochemical balance needed to function. But medication alone cannot be the total answer. Truly effective treatment of prolonged despair is not quick-fix hospitalization, injections to restore deficient hormones, and anti-depressant drugs. Spiritual activity along with natural disposition, medical attention, proper diet, and regular exercise are essential to a happy outlook.

Again, characters from *Pilgrim's Progress* can remind us of the value of prayer. Christian and Hopeful broke loose from the dread Doubting Castle. Giant Despair, along with his wife Diffidence, ran Doubting Castle. Their deliverance was told as follows:

> ...on Saturday about midnight, [Christian and Hopeful] began to pray, and continued in prayer till almost break of day. Now, a little before it was day, good Christian, as one half amazed, brake out into this passionate speech: "What a fool...am I, thus to lie in a stinking dungeon, when I may as well walk at liberty! I have a key in my bosom, called Promise, that will, I am persuaded, open any lock in Doubting Castle." Then said Hopeful, "That's good news, good brother, pluck it out of thy bosom, and try." Then Christian pulled it out of his bosom, and began to try at the dungeon door, whose bolt, as he turned the key, gave back, and the door flew open with ease, and Christian and Hopeful both came out.[20]

WINNING WAYS

• No sense arguing with the aging process. It can't be permanently stopped. (But it can be slowed!) Get reconciled with your loss of youth and lean into the blessings of mature years.

• Despair saps our drive and desire. Through a physician's care, hormone depletions can be supplemented. But even when our bodies are functioning at their peak, such as young athletes, we are never completely spared weakness. Even youthful vigor will falter, but those who wait on the Lord shall renew their strength. They shall mount up with wings as eagles, they shall run and not be weary, they shall walk and not faint (Isa. 40:30, 31 KJV).

• Prayer helps produce tranquility and keep our immune system strong. But medical knowledge can be used by God to make the transition into the problems of seniorhood a little easier. Hormone therapy, such as estrogen, has been known to transform some from being nasty into being nice.

• Review the five ways to overcome despair in this chapter.

THINGS TO THINK ABOUT:

[1] Discuss how depression comes to us. What can give you "the blues"?

[2] In bereavement, depression is often a delayed reaction. When has depression been strongest in your experience? What kind of self-grieving helped you most to cope? What portions of Scripture helped you the most?

[3] Did the prospect of retirement scare you? pain you? annoy you? or revive you? Are retirees happier or sadder than those who work to their life's end?

[4] What expectations do you have if you are not yet retired? If you are retired, has despair made its appearance? How do you plan to meet a depression's reappearance?

[5] Beyond personal disappointment, loss, and despair, Christians can be bothered by false guilt. Does false guilt contribute to depression? To what degree does biochemical imbalance in depression get blamed as spiritual degeneration? How does one distinguish between physiological needs and spiritual failure?

14

TEMPTED TO SUICIDE

Old age hath yet his honor and his toil;
Death closes all: but something ere the end,
Some work of note may yet be done.[1]
                              —Alfred Lord Tennyson

Creative and recreative activity can occupy senior leisure so that end-of-day fulfillments outdo end-of-life
complaints. Aesthetic enjoyments can offset increased
physical ailments. Sherwood Eliot Wirt, former editor
of *Decision* magazine, challenged negative estimates of
the senior season:

> …old age is the best time of life. It is what happened to
> me. Ask me whether life is better at eighty than it was at
> forty. Ask me whether I am more in tune with the
> environment, more appreciative of my blessings, more
> delighted at what each day brings, more interested in
> what I am doing than I was when I was younger. Ask
> me whether the vision is as strong now as it was when
> it first came to me. [2]

And yet, for too many seniors there is a dark—very
dark—side of our situation that tempts us to consider…
suicide. How can suicide be a temptation? When life is

good, we wish to continue in it, to promote it, cherish it, lengthen and protect it. Some enthusiasts for life consider anyone contemplating suicide tragically "tetched." That conclusion may be too cavalier. Attempts at suicide may be a result from the grip of self-torture. After all, some non-psychotics do choose suicide.

SUICIDES AMONG SENIORS

Volume 2 (Mortality) of *Vital Statistics of the United States* (Department of Health, Education, and Welfare) Public Health Services indicates that senior adult white males have a high incidence of suicide. For our purposes it is enough to recognize from public health data that seniors show an unusually high percentage of suicides. The facts are astonishing. Here is an uncomfortable summary:

> Americans over sixty-five are nearly twice as likely to take their own lives as the rest of the population...nearly 30 percent of suicides in the U. S. are in the [over sixty] age group....Though the elderly make up only 11 percent of the population, they account for one-fourth of all suicides. [3]

WHAT IS SUICIDE?

Scots Presbyterian Thomas Guthrie [1803-1873] speculated that most adults "commit suicide of sort through their neglect of the ordinary rules of health, or the injudicious use of meat, drink, or medicine."[4] Guthrie considered overindulgence in food, drink, or drugs passive suicide. Guthrie hit upon a central dynamic in suicide: self-hate. Excesses usually show an attempt to annihilate oneself because self is disliked, even hated. Pre-suicide counseling and post-suicide evidence (e.g. notes left by the deceased) indicate assorted angers turned inward lead to the end effect.

Many aspects of suicide are untouched on these pages. The subject is complex. We refer to recent developments that encourage readers to be cautious in being super judgmental. Three assumptions or axioms are the basis of what follows.

1. Suicide generally is an intentional act of self-destruction;
2. Christianity is traditionally opposed to active suicide;
3. Patient choice to cease prolonged life-support treatment is not suicide.

We leave some important questions unexplored, such as whether suicides are ever accidental, what constitutes physician assistance of suicide, and issues related to the permanently unconscious patient. Anyone wishing to deal with morality issues in euthanasia is encouraged to read the excellent work by Robert N. Wennberg.[5] Another work worth consulting is the more recent, shorter work by James T. Clemons.[6]

CONVENTIONAL WISDOM ON SUICIDE

Many civil libertarians view self-chosen suicide as the ultimate act of free speech. Faced with overwhelming loss, many take the attitude that better a terrible end than no end of terribleness. A terminally ill cancer patient in full control of his mind may reason that he is ending his dying more than ending his life. In self-justification some seniors figure suicide expedites God's decision to reclaim a life.

Physician-assisted suicide for those suffering from advanced Alzheimer's disease, advanced multiple sclerosis, and other serious maladies continues to be widely debated. One octogenarian suffering from Parkinson's disease said, "I'd pay somebody to take me behind the barn and shoot me but [Dr. Kevorkian's death machine] sounds a lot neater."[7]

The prolongation of a spent life seemed senseless to physician-trained novelist Somerset Maugham [1874-1965]. At sixty-four, he approved of suicide: "I can only approve the man who makes an end to himself of his own will when life has nothing to offer him but pain and misfortune."[8]

When life is near being closed down, some elders wish to implement God's recall by the least disgusting method. They reason that it makes no sense to clutter life's highway with broken-down vehicles. Why jam history's path with "rust bucket" bodies, goes the reasoning, when able-bodied travelers are waiting their turn and need to pass?

Profound questions have been raised whether suicide is ever justified. Why artificially prolong a spent body? Why should states permit abortions yet regard physician-assisted suicides of the terminally ill as illegal? How can prolonging the life of persons in a vegetative state be of permanent value? Isn't extending life under such circumstances as bad as stopping it at the beginning? If it is a constitutional right to get into this world, does it not follow one has the same right to exit?

These questions also relate to physician-assisted suicides. Are lethal injections for the terminally ill unfair, inhumane, and immoral? Into the "throw-in-the-towel arena" has entered a retired (and unlicensed) Michigan pathologist, Dr. Jack Kevorkian. Dr. Kevorkian has unashamedly assisted in a variety of self-chosen suicides. Whether he is a public benefactor or medical "loose cannon" on the pitching deck of life is not at issue here. Physician-assisted suicide is a heated debate by medical ethicists. At present in Michigan and several other states, there is a movement to make assisted suicides criminal. Some fear that the "suicide doctor" has given Michigan a reputation as the "suicide state."

WHAT PREDISPOSES A PERSON
TO SUICIDAL THOUGHTS?

Walking through thicket-thick arguments will not leave us without scratches. Although over-indulgence and bodily abuses increase prospects for an early death, they fail to meet the usual criteria of "suicide." Unconsciously provoking slow suicide can hardly be used to justify conscious suicide. Death by degrees is no argument in favor of active suicide or assisted suicide. An attending physician who increases dosage of morphine to a terminally ill cancer patient is not promoting or assisting a suicide. A side effect of massive morphine injections puts a patient at risk of fatal respiratory arrest. Yet none of the attending medical staff in the hospital or hospice is guilty of assisting a suicide. The point is not that suicide is right, but that one cannot label as "suicide" every decision that ends in death. The key, according to Robert Wennberg, is whether or not an act is *intentionally* suicidal. Most health-care professionals do not consider cessation of treatment or morphine shots as aiding and abetting suicide.

One characteristic of aging is a growing inability to connect the dots between chronological dates and feeling one's age. In her fourth autobiography, Simone de Beauvoir spoke for many when she wrote:

> Like everybody else, I am incapable of an inner experience of it: age is one of the things that cannot be realized. Seeing that my health is good, my body gives me no token of age. I am sixty-three: and this truth remains foreign to me.[9]

SUICIDE MAKERS

One way to avoid falling for suicide is to avoid its two sharpest curves: The first curve is to lose interest in living right. That occurs early on. The reckless spirit, the feeling of invincibility, and the belief one can dodge dissipation after wanton disregard of the body heads one down a pre-suicidal path. A passive suicidal attitude precedes its active suicidal version.

The second curve that leads to suicide is much sharper: It is to lose interest in living—period. When health begins to collapse, suicide may seem to be the easiest solution. The shock of failed body parts is what throws some seniors into a depression that, in turn, encourages contemplation of suicide. The grim prospect of irreversible organ failures can make suicide alluring. Too much emphasis on good health and physical wellness profoundly affects some desires to exit. Seniors are less concerned about the ten plagues of Egypt (cf. The Book of Exodus) than the seven plagues of the elderly:

insomnia	isolation
incontinence	insolvency
impotence	immobility
indigestion	

One reason many seniors are tempted to see suicide as less an evil and more a good is that most make their own medical choices. They presume that their condition is beyond fixing, beyond correcting, beyond reversing, beyond recovery. That sets them up to lower their guard against tempting thoughts of suicide. Retreat from life is a dangerous state of mind. In isolation from sound medical consultation, the worst conclusions are inferred. Lonely detachment, in Sherwood Wirt's words, "invite the Devil in for a field day. Anything can happen."[10]

Giving up on our bodies compounds human despair. Gradual deterioration in organ function or joints can entice some one to reject replacement parts. New surgical interventions—hip and knee replacements, for example—can prolong and improve one's quality of life.

Many welcome radical surgeries to extend their lives. Abandoning our body parts' durability is premature. When an eighty-four-year-old man in the care of his adult children is too proud to continue living with his incontinence, he may take out his false teeth and refuse to eat so he can die. In his mind he is sparing his family humiliation and aggravations. Dr. Koop, the former U.S. Surgeon General, noted, "Few Americans realize that most urinary incontinence is easy to treat, even cure."[11]

PRESUMPTIONS AND SUICIDE

A key deterrent to suicide is to avoid a series of erroneous assumptions. Presumption is the primary self-killer. Rationalizations for suicide are replete with presumptions. Some even mistakenly think that suicide can bring one closer to God, sooner! There also is the notion that suicide moves one from a bad life to a better one, from primary state of pain to an advanced state of pleasure. But suicide does not exchange human complexity and mortality for a simpler, easier eternal life. Reading and believing Scripture challenges, corrects, and changes our assumptions about life and the afterlife. Belief that post-death existence is necessarily simpler, grander, and more fulfilling—for everyone—is unsupported by the Bible.

Presumption is a powerful predisposing factor in many of many, if not most, suicide cases. Various studies over many years indicate that prospective suicides feel abandoned and, therefore, give up on living. Depression due to perceived neglect seems to mean nonexistence has already begun. The leap in this logic is that there is no change between life later from life now. Better the loss of life, the potential suicide victim feels than the continuation of a living death of being ignored and unappreciated. So, mild depression becomes acute.

It seems Ernest Hermingway's impotence prodded him to first seek suicide by walking into an airplane propeller in Casper, Wyoming, and then, later, to use a shotgun in Idaho. According to psychologist Rollo May, Ernest Hemingway's suicide was driven by his impotence.[12]

Some males incline toward suicide when their sexual capabilities diminish or disappear. The loss of sex drive is taken as a reason to leave this life. Thoughts of death can dominate when an activity that was one of life's better experiences is gone; purpose for living can evaporate. Some males hope testosterone patches, penile injections or other methods will rejuvenate their sexual potency. The most promising procedure now seems to be oral medication.[13]

> Old age should be a time for integration of the whole life experience, for fulfillment. Yet for so many it becomes a time of self-disgust and despair. The disgust comes from no longer being able to produce and be useful….The despair is a form of chronic depression that is acted out in a high rate of suicide among those over sixty-five.[14]

Suicide is wrong in part because it prevents life from being longer. Self-murder deprives us of the joy of engaging in new discoveries and noteworthy relationships. False presumption can push a senior to think his life is essentially over when it is probably far from it. The wrongness of suicide, however, lies primarily in that it violates God's revealed will in the Commandment regarding our stewardship of God-given life.

An indelible impression was made on me about how medical "comebacks" are possible with the elderly. My first New Testament Greek professor in seminary was the late Dr. George Handy Wailes. He was teaching both at Philadelphia Theological Seminary and Temple Uni-

versity School of Theology following his mandatory
retirement from Princeton Seminary. Sometime in his
late seventies, Dr. Wailes had colon cancer surgery. But
he lived on for twenty more years—into his nineties—
still teaching Greek!

Old age in humans is like old ice on earth. Naturalists
know that snow's existence does not end with the return
of spring. There are four stages beyond initial snow:

> snow turns to aging snow
> aging snow turns to ice
> ice turns to ancient ice
> ancient ice turns to glacial ice.

Glacial ice carved out the valleys in Wyoming's Grand
Teton Mountain range. Glacial ice sculpted the beauti-
ful rock shapes of California's Sierra Madre Mountains.
Leave thoughts on the origin of mountain ranges for a
moment and think of the shaping and creative products
of Frank Lloyd Wright who, at age eighty-eight, de-
signed California's Marin County Civic Center. Or consider Leopold Stokowski who signed a six-year record-
ing contract at age ninety-four.[15] Sister Teresa still advanced her Nobel prize-winning work until days before
her death at eighty-eight. Age is no excuse to give up
productive living.

DISBELIEF IN GOD: ANOTHER SUICIDE MAKER

Non-Christian philosophies often seem sympathetic toward suicide. In their eyes there is no God—the creator
of Life—to whom they must answer. Therefore, many
have no philosophical objections to suicide. Seneca, the
Roman Stoic, argued "As I choose the ship in which I
will sail, and the house I will inhabit, so I will choose the
death by which I will leave life."

Empiricist David Hume [1711-1776] posed a similar
point: "It would be no crime in me to divert the Nile or

Danube from its course, were I able to effect such purposes. Where, then, is the crime of turning a few ounces
of blood from their natural course."

The French existentialist novelist Albert Camus [1913-
1960] died prematurely in an auto accident. He saw no
meaning in life except in one's own experience. To
Camus both life and death fulfill nothing. His philosophy left followers with ambivalent feelings about death,
to say the least. He was for living but only for the sake of
living, and death was only a trap door through which
we drop to nothingness. Shorn of Christian belief in
resurrection, the non-Christian existentialist holds that
no purpose is served after death. Without purposes to
be served after death, how could he/she object to suicide?

The Christian, however, has "a sure and certain hope"
both in life and in death. The Christian understands,
believes, and finds strength from the view that he knows
both by whom and for whom he was made—and through
whom we receive the gift of eternal life. The Lord who
gives natural life also grants supernatural life. Both are
gifts. The Lord who initiates life accompanies, supports,
maintains, and preserves life. God of the Ages is our
timeless comfort, companion, savior, and friend.

The God who creates also gives guidance in His
Word. For example, the Giver of life revealed His will in
the Commandment "Thou shalt not kill" (literally: murder). "Only God, consequently, is entitled to determine
when and how life is to end."[16] In His Word, God gives
us incentives to keep going even when life seems as
bumpy, uneven, and rutted as a dirt road up a distant
mountain. To cut short one's life cancels God's promise
to show His power in delivering us from evil outcomes.
Carrying out a suicide is deciding for God, not just for
the victim. Cowardice—more than courage—usually
prevails in the suicidal urge. But the Lord's own are

enabled to wait for interventions, reversals, and miraculous recoveries. Psalm 66:9-12, NIV, reflects that willingness:

> Praise our God, O peoples, let the sound of his praise be heard; he has preserved our lives and kept our feet from slipping. For you, O God, tested us; You brought us into prison and laid burdens on our backs. You let men ride over our heads; we went through fire and water, but you brought us to a place of abundance.

SUICIDE IS MURDER

Suicide reflects low-level spirituality rather than a high-level rational option. Suicide is a clumsy, unnecessarily cruelty—to ourselves and loved ones—and a desperate attempt to escape mental or physical pain and inner conflicts. Once a person understands what lies beneath impulses toward self-destruction, the grip of a suicide option should loosen. We know not nearly enough, but still too much, about suicide to be deceived by claims for its civility or sanity. Behind most suicides lurks self-hate, and beneath self-hate often lies rage—anger to the nth degree—to "get even" with someone. One way to prevent suicide is to uncover that rage and confront the anger.

Frequently, murderers turn the fatal weapon upon themselves. That reaction goes beyond belief that the culprit feared prosecution. Such murderers are driven by a boiling rage resembling that of suicides. Tragically, the murderer is also killing those targeted by his/her own suicidal rage. A pastor friend told of a grieving question asked by the parents of a teenage suicide: "Why didn't he kill us, too, while he was at it? He just as well might have."

What factors try to justify suicidal acts? How do they develop? From our perspective, suicide is driven by a mental merger. A person's capacity for intense, deep, and lasting identification with another person flips from love and admiration to the opposite side of hate and need to destroy. Secretly motivating some suicides is the wish to punish a dominant person in one's life. Like murder, suicide expresses the wish to rid oneself of that person(s), to finally stop their despised interferences, control, and lack of appreciation. A person can be killing himself when he fantasizes that he is really killing the person he hates. This hatred provides the emotional energy to carry through on the desire to punish or ruin that person.

> Rage is the most common hidden reason for suicide; expressed honesty can be the best medicine to cure this impulse.

Projection is an advanced state of presumption. In murdering self, the suicide may get some satisfaction in hurting someone else, even someone physically absent. Lucy Freeman summarized this sentiment:

> …The suicide kills (forever loses) that part of himself identified with the loved/hated one as he turns on himself his overwhelming guilt because of his murderous wishes….Suicides often have the conscious fantasy of revenge on the lost loved one just before they kill themselves.[17]

BRIGHTENING GLOOM

Wanting to live has much to do with feeling wanted. The high rate of suicide among the elderly is due, in many instances, to failing to feel valued. A friend's mother-in-law, whose heart finally failed at age ninety-five, had overcome numerous health setbacks over the previous decade that would have ended others' lives in large part because she knew how much her daughter (his wife) valued her.

Joshua, Moses' successor in leading Israel, faced the problem of having his body quit on him. Midway through the book of Joshua he retired from military service (13:1). It was understandable that at age one hundred his military career was over. God told him what still had to be done. God valued Joshua and gave him new work. He was less retired than redirected.

Obviously, God did not consider Joshua totally washed up, finished, unneeded. Though God no longer wanted him to raise his spear, Joshua was to raise his voice. He turned from being a military strategist to becoming a real estate broker when God appointed Joshua to parcel out the newly conquered land of Canaan among the twelve tribes of Israel. After that was done, Joshua was to give two major speeches: One to the tribal elders (Chapter 23) and then to the entire nation (Chapter 24), which he did in his 110th year (24:29). Joshua could have thought it was all over when it became difficult for him to see the enemy or to draw and wield his sword to any effect. When physical disabilities or deterioration descend upon us in our senior years, we can be tempted to quit life. Joshua' close relationship with God kept him ready to continue and willing to work. After all, throughout Israel's wandering in the wilderness, God had been at work to forge twelve squabbling tribes into a unified nation. If Joshua had quit—"Hey, Lord, I'm too old for this"—all that work could have come undone via tribal conflicts over who got what territory in the Promised Land.

Life can be restarted (some would say reinvented) by turning misfortunes into meaningful futures. For example, the first snowmobile originally was a toboggan with two skies in front. In 1924, Carl Eliason of Sayner, Wisconsin said, "I was too old to keep up with my buddies when we went out to tend trap lines." A motorized traction belt on the toboggan part was the difference. His first major order was from Finland for two hundred snowmobiles. He sold his patent to a Clintonville, Wisconsin company. One of their first orders was for three hundred snowmobiles for the U. S. military.

Another example: In the 1930s a Minneapolis boy named John Kormylo slipped along the railroad tracks and a freight train ran over his foot. In time his leg was amputated below the knee. His disability turned into an advantage for others with similar limb loss, because John Kormylo was motivated to learn how to make artificial limbs. Because of asthma he had to move to drier climate. He settled in a northern Wyoming town (Thermopolis) that sits on a series of year-round hot bubbling mineral springs. Working from the Gottsche Rehabilitation Center at Thermopolis, Kormyulo became a world-renowned prosthetics expert. He has fitted artificial limbs for all sorts of people of all ages: 75,000 individually crafted artificial limbs (17,000 of which were devices for maimed U. S. servicemen).[18]

We should put an exclamation point on each year past sixty. Then do our best to pack new achievements into each fold of those years. That's the way to finish life!

Eighty-year-old missionary-statesman Robert E. Speer [1867-1947] wrote a touching greeting on the eightieth birthday of Dr. Samuel M. Zwemer [1867-1952], the famous Christian missionary to Islam.[19]

> My dear Sam:
>   So this week on Saturday you will be four score—and thank God it is not 'labor and sorrow' but 'work and joy.'...A fourscore blessing! I can imagine God saying: 'This is my dear, true, powerful servant, Sam. He is one of my best and bravest. Angels, take special care of him! Let no harm come to him. Breathe his mind and heart full of power.' That is my prayer for you, dearest old friend. —Robert E. Speer

Zwemer had retired in 1951 at the age of eighty-four. In the same year he put together and had published his last book, the insightful *Sons of Adam.*

Age need not block us from productive work. We seniors have much left in us for God's glory, mission, and ministry. Break loose from a fixation on what we did during the last three decades. Rather focus on new possibilities in the next three years. Like Joshua at one hundred, greet the challenges in the new opportunities. Our bodies may have aches and pains we did not feel thirty years ago, but we should not lose our desire to keep active in ways that are possible for us. This drive inspired Sherwood Wirt to write:

> Don't treat us the way the world treats us! Put us to work, please. Set us to praying, teaching, building, cooking, feeding, clothing, serving on committees, going on deputations, working on budgets, exhorting, singing, playing instruments, entertaining, sewing, writing, broadcasting, lecturing on tours, leading home fellowships—whatever seems to fit our capabilities and qualifications. Just don't segregate us permanently into a Golden Age group and make us into a pale imitation of life.[20]

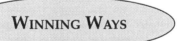

WINNING WAYS

• Suicide is the ultimate "I quit." Better to battle back from troubles than to regard self-murder as a solution. Christians should resist throwing in the towel because, even in our latter years, we can give witness to God's past and continuous grace and goodness.

• Suicidal thoughts entice to suicidal actions. The key to not succumbing to suicide is keeping in contact with Christ in His Word, and in contact with others in His household of faith.

• Suicidal thoughts usually are disguised rage. Deal with sources of that rage. Christians have good reasons to live. It takes more courage to stay than to leave.

Although one sphere of our influence may shrink, God can use us in other ways where now there seems to be no purpose.

• Avoid making the mistake of cutting short God's ability to use us our senior years. Keep your oars in the water. See yourself as being experienced enough to help show others how to face transitions. Let the impact of your eventual end be a powerful message of the goodness of God.

THINGS TO THINK ABOUT:

[1] Are you familiar with some suicide cases? Briefly review known details and, at a distance that makes indiscreet revelation impossible, venture to estimate what appeared to be some contributing causes.

[2] Some Christians have been harshly judgmental on all suicides—i.e., the centuries-old policy of burying suicides either outside church cemetery fences or with their tombstones facing west. Is it possible for Christians to fall into thinking their intentional premature death could accomplish a good purpose? What about the case of Samson (Judges 16:28-31)? Was his death suicide? St. Augustine held that Samson's heroic death was evil.[21] Does Scripture make a judgment on Samson regarding his unusual exit? How could Samson make it into Hebrews 11:32?

[3] There seems to be a hierarchy of choices in the self-chosen suicide: reckless but unexpected death; not really intended accidental death but desired accidental death; expected self-death; desired and intended death. Do these cover all options?

[4] Does where one fits in this hierarchy determine whether an apparent suicide is intentional self-murder?

15

TEMPTED TO
PUT OFF

Though I look old, yet I am strong and lusty;
For in my youth I never did apply
Hot and rebellious liquors in my blood,
Nor did not with unbashful forehead woo
The means of weakness and debility;
Therefore my age is as a lusty winter,
Frosty, but kindly: let me go with you;
I'll do the service of a younger man
In all your business and necessities.[1]
—Shakespeare

Why wait to do good? Propitious moments to show kindness and volunteer to help those in need should be seized when the opportunity arises. Thank God, seniors constitute a huge volunteer force. Many cheerfully respond to urgent calls for intervention. And many also anticipate needs for caregiving by funding professional services that alleviate personal suffering.

Although seniors can't put off aging, they can put off indecision. Postponed action can guarantee troubles later. Every delayed action, each indecision snarls life's enjoyment!

Retirement doesn't lengthen time. Time has its own pace. We can recharge and redirect how time works for us when, as the Psalmist says, "My times are in thy hands." This attitude opens up new ventures and opportunities, and we are freed to pursue avocations. Enchanting places to visit await us, marvelous books to read, favorite hobbies to develop, lost sleep to regain, and for some the chance to play chess any weeknight.

During the Vietnam War several dozen members of the National Procrastinators Club picketed Philadelphia's City Hall carrying signs protesting…the War of 1812: "President Madison —This is Your War!" Allegedly, when one of its members died, his wife honored the club and concept, if not the man, with this epitaph:

> He walked beneath the moon;
> He slept beneath the sun;
> He lived the life of 'going to do,'
> And died with nothing done!

Would we qualify for the National Procrastinators Club, belatedly begun in 1952? Most seniors I know are too busy to join. Actually, no duly inducted member ever joins when he said he would. And none of the members pay their dues on time. If they did, they'd be thrown out.

When we love life, we have reason to put off death. We'd like to bribe death to hold off endlessly, if we could. No sense being in a hurry to go to heaven, even Christians reason, since Christ has already brought something of heaven to us on earth. Some mature adults put off retirement plans. Unfortunately, because of lack of foresight and failure to anticipate the cost of travel, many stay at home, left with lovely dreams that never become realities. For octogenarians, making plans too far ahead can be foolish. Presbyterian pastor Morgan Phelps Noyes confessed as he neared eighty, "When you get to be almost eighty you can't plan thirty years ahead very well, although it's surprising how little you think about there being a termination."[2]

Procrastinators inhabit all age groups, including seniors. British Lord Chesterfield [1694-1773] was a case in point. He had the nerve to exhort his son—"Never put off till tomorrow what you can do today"—yet he never got around to marrying his son's mother. He also had this inconsiderate habit of keeping notables, such as Dr. Ben Johnson, left waiting and perspiring under wigs in an anteroom.

Many veterans have clear memories of how slowly military processing lines moved. The slogan "Hurry up and wait" had special meaning to them. Lawyers, usually prompt in preparing wills for clients, are sometimes the worst procrastinators. According to one Beverly Hills insurance salesman, "The number of attorneys who die without a will is amazing."

POSTPONEMENT PASSES AWAY

Once action on procrastinated matters is finally taken, hedging has stopped. But beware. When delayed ambitions are finally enjoyed, new kinds of procrastination may emerge.

> The people who seem to weather old age the best and live longest seem to be the ones who have planned ahead. A person should not regard as inevitable the prospect of a useless and lonely old age. Instead, he should plan on useful and satisfying activities for his post-retirement years and maintain strong links to friends and family.[3]

Alibis for indecision can put streaks of cowardly yellow in otherwise pure white hair. Retirement does not render us suddenly incompetent, but it can sap our confidence, especially about what we can yet do, learn, try, and become. Too many of us feel uneasy about making new tracks in the untrammeled snows of advancing age. Options for making fresh goals and seeking new frontiers can frighten and freeze us. Broad smiles return to seniors, however, when they discover that their hesitation arose more from nagging inferiority complexes than from real inadequacies.

WHAT REALLY LIES BEHIND PROCRASTINATION?

"Garfield" in cat food commercials tries to justify his inaction. When accused of listlessness, the TV commercial has him quickly deny the charge by saying, "No, not listless, just an advanced stage of relaxation." If we want absolute relaxation, death offers it.

We are most often not undone, but not doing. Russian novelist, Leo Tolstoy [1828-1910] was vigorous even when very old. He learned to ride a bicycle at age sixty-seven without abandoning horseback riding and hiking.[4] Jeanne Calment, the world's oldest person at the time, died at age 122. She took up fencing at age eighty-five and still rode a bicycle at one hundred.[5]

Some of the most successful public figures have been unable to enjoy their successes in senior years. Some may identify with Benjamin Disraeli [1804-1881], England's Prime Minister throughout much of the Victorian era. Despite a vitriolic manner in his later years, Disraeli enjoyed widespread political support. He also championed the Athanasian Creed as "the most splendid ecclesiastical lyric ever poured forth by the genius of man." Unfortunately, Disraeli had a dismal outlook even at forty when he wrote "Youth is a mistake, manhood a struggle, and old age a regret." Gouty and asthmatic he vented another vinegar confession at age seventy-seven: "I have known something of action in my life; it is a life of baffled hopes and wasted energies."[6] Rather than rejoice in God's goodness, Disraeli's put-down of life's happy moments can strike us as railing against St. Paul's admiration of "things of good report."

No one can absolve Disraeli's gloom. We can imitate the action of less literate but talented artists Giovanni Bellini in his seventies and Rembrandt in his sixties. By their examples, these two men from two different countries and eras effectively X-ed out Disraeli's pessimism, for they painted some of their greatest works in their sixties and seventies, an age when a sour Disraeli whined. Far more people are lifted by contemplating these artists' works than are scared off by Disraeli's acid language. Take them as models for senior participation. Life can finish with a magnificent flourish. Whenever we feel a lazy streak coming on to darken our spirit, override it by declaring the Latin slogan: *carpe diem* ("seize the day").

Inaction is sometimes rationalized as "ambivalence," although the latter involves choices that are not clear cut. There is more to indecision than emotional inertia. Pro-crastination's problem is that it short-circuits the value of action. According to many psychologists, procrastination overflows with hidden contempt, using ambivalence as an excuse to ride a bubble. It stuffs life's envelope with blank checks by allowing ambivalence to pose as a philosophical pillow. The incessantly lethargic should ask themselves whether their irresolution actually stems from laziness.

The medieval church ranked procrastination among the seven deadly sins. They called it "Acadia." In the twelfth-century *acadia* meant to fail to be sufficiently active in pursuit of recognized Good. It acknowledged the Good, but did not seek it. The first step to conquering procrastination is to see it as a terrible habit before we'll have to admit it is a "damning" sin.

WHAT MAKES PROCRASTINATION A HABIT?

Procrastination is a nasty habit rather than a dirty one. In the snore of the sluggard, there often is a psychological scream that is not a call for rescue but an expression of a troubled spirit. The two most common components of procrastination are hidden anger and secret fear. Chronically late arrivals point to a deep-down power play of showing "who's boss." A person "never on time" is making that clearer than he or she realizes.

Young people have a reputation for putting off. In the eighteenth century, Bible commentator Matthew Henry [1662-1714] thought it nothing short of pernicious for young people to "get a habit of sauntering."[7] Today, many of them seem so "laid back" one can wonder whether they secretly wish to be "laid out." Society also helps excuse inaction by calling it "leisure time" when it may be, instead, a perpetuation of unresolved protest from one's earlier years. Psychologists refer to delayed obedience and "late-arrival-itus" as forms of passive aggression. Adult indecision also may be a carry over from negative reactions to domineering parents.[8]

Our psyches use many strategies to escape guilt. One is to let hyperactivity in one area (whether in physical or mental activity) salve our conscience for being lazy in another. So we end our days playing tricks on our conscience. But when lazy, we often are motivated by a hidden anger.

> There was an old sailor my grandfather knew,
> Who had so many things which he wanted to do,
> That whenever he thought it was time to begin,
> He couldn't, because of the state he was in.
>
> —Author Unknown

TWO COMMON PRESUMPTIONS TO AVOID

Presumption #1: Life will continue unchanged

In our sixties, even into our seventies and eighties, death seems distant—unless the death of someone near to us makes us very conscious of our own mortality. Nevertheless, "swift to its close ebbs out life's little day" (Henry Lyte). We cannot be absolutely sure about tomorrow, of course. What will happen the next day is impossible to know. Although as seniors we understandably desire stability zones in our lives, we cannot be sure life—as we know it—will continue unchanged.

Presumption #2: Haste is always a vice

Some put off action lest it be viewed as ill-considered haste. Consider how the prophet Isaiah chided Israel: "You hurry down to Egypt without consulting me" (3:2 NEB). Proverbs 21:5 (NEB) warns "The man in a hurry is sure to poverty." Proverbs also warns against being quick tempered (14:29). A quick tongue (25:8) is often hair-triggered (1:16; 21:5). Hamlet was not alone in regarding haste as bad ("O wicked speed to post with such dexterity to incestuous sheets..."). Genesis described God, after Adam and Eve's eating the forbidden fruit, as strolling through the Garden "in the cool of the day" (Gen. 3:8). Note: God was not huffing through the vegetation to slay the two transgressors. After all, God is slow to anger (Nahum 1:3). His promises are fulfilled without delay, although at times they seem to be tardy, placed "on hold."

Seniors should not neglect getting involved in "so great a salvation" (Heb. 2:3). God has written the musical term "presto" (as fast as possible) over every gospel invitation. Because faith, obedience, and submission to Christ are necessary, Richard Baxter [1615-1691] urged: "What speed should such a people make for heaven!

How should they fly, that are thus winged! And how swiftly should they sail, that have wind and tide to help them!"[9]

RESULTS OF SPIRITUAL IDLENESS

On several occasions, Jesus spoke of the perils of delay (Matt. 5:25-26; 13:45-46; Mark 4:28-29; Luke 16:3). If God takes our deferrals as denials, what then?

A house left idle (Matt. 12:44) was ripe for demonic occupancy. Empty niceness will not keep Satan from exercising squatter's rights (Matt. 23:21). On the premise that idleness is not only a sin but fertile ground for the growth of wickedness, senior years can become an ideal time for Satan to harvest evil. So, the Epistle to the Hebrews comes down hard on spiritual laxity (cf. 3:12-13; 6:11-12; 12:12). John Calvin observed: "Many sinners, intoxicated with the pleasures of vice, think not of the judgment of God. Lying stupefied, as it were, by a kind of lethargy, they aspire not to the offered mercy."[10]

Still a favorite with many Christians, second only to the Bible, is John Bunyan's *Pilgrim's Progress* is one of the bestselling book of all time. Perhaps least known was his allegory "The Heavenly Footman." Its aim was to shame people out of dragging their heels to fellowship with God. "…no greater shame can befall a man than to see that he hath fooled away his soul, and sinned away eternal life."[11]

> Let not conscience make you linger
> Nor of fitness fondly dream;
> All the fitness He requires
> Is to feel your need of Him.
> —Joseph Hart [1712-1768]

WHAT TO DO ABOUT PROCRASTINATION

There is a strong tendency to put off change until a crisis necessitates it. It is far better to move aggressively and early.[12]

"Things to do before it is too late" should include such things as age-proofing the house, establishing good nutritional habits, and preparing a will. A "do list" should include:

[1] See your physician

Annual complete physicals make sense for catching a health problem early rather than letting it develop into a major catastrophe. Many seniors would benefit from earlier medical intervention. By putting off blood analysis, medications, or surgical correction of a problem, their condition can become too advanced to provide successful treatment. If the money doesn't seem to be there for regular physicals, it's time to reexamine priorities and reallocate whatever is available.

[2] Exercise

Before attempting vigorous forms of exercise, consult your physician. For some, taking up tennis may not be advisable, for example. One of the features of remaining a home owner for as long as possible is that there is always something to do, to fix, to clean, to paint, to plant, and to rearrange. Yard work and gardening provide exercise benefits. Walking the dog helps your pet and you.

[3] Make key arrangements

As we age, we may need to find housing where maintenance is paid for. Knowing our real options in housing and financial management are important.

Have you made a will? A living will on how to handle a dependency state should be considered, too.[13] Consulting a lawyer with other family members may be wise. In such consultation, how dependency will be handled in the event of your incapacitation should be specified. Procrastinate in legal/fiscal areas and much of your estate could be devoured by probate and unnecessary taxes.

Of course, make fiscal arrangements after determining what will be left to distribute. Some seniors make funeral arrangements long before their health fails. For instance, one of my sisters-in-law, eventually taken by bone cancer, prearranged her funeral. That was her way of freeing the family to engage in mutual support and prayer.

Don't let approaching death immobilize you. Take hold of what future God grants you. Be as productive as you can each day. We feel good about living when we do good things for ourselves and others. Plan ahead. Prioritize what needs immediate attention. Make sure the projects are not overly demanding and anticipate logistical problems. Use some of your savings, if need be, to maintain your health. Your beneficiaries will do just fine without the dollars it costs you to enjoy a good quality of life.

RETIREMENT IS A TIME FOR ACTION

Ever watch snails? They travel slowly—some at just 198 inches per hour. Others have been clocked at two inches per minute, or .009 m.p.h. The fastest snail was measured in the Costa Rica mountains at 18 inches a minute or .017 m.p.h.[14] Procrastination makes us move even slower than snails.

Personal devotions have been influenced by our culture's stress on speed. Consequently, too many Christians zip through devotional readings. Others creep through them. What all of us need is a vigorous, sustained Bible reading program to improve our spiritual health. Familiarize yourself with each book's themes, development, and key features. There are several study Bibles specifically geared to seniors.[15]

Prayer can be as important as Bible reading. Pray

while reading Scripture. Without responding to God while reading hinders our inhaling Scripture's invigorating oxygen. Prayer encourages us to engage with God's Word more personally.

> I met God in the morning,
> When my day was at its best,
> And his presence came like sunrise,
> Like his glory in my breast.
> And I think of other mornings,
> When a keen remorse of mind,
> When I too had loosed the moorings,
> With the presence left behind.
> So l think I know the secret
> Learned from many a troubled way,
> You must meet him in the morning,
> If you want Him through the day.[16]
>   —Ralph S. Cushman

Business world eager beavers are unlike do-nothing, sit-tight church members. There is something pitiful about a life in bud that never blossoms. Such a person is described in these lines—

He was going to be all that he wanted to be—Tomorrow.
None would be kinder or braver than he—Tomorrow.
A friend who was traveled and weary he knew,
Who'd be glad for a lift and who needed it too.
On him he would call and see what he could do—Tomorrow.
Each morning he'd stack up the letters he'd write—Tomorrow.
And thought of the folks he would fill with delight—Tomorrow.
And hadn't one minute to stop on his way
"More time I will have to give others"—Tomorrow.
The greatest of workers this man could have been—Tomorrow.
The world would have hailed him had he seen—Tomorrow.
But in fact, he passed on and faded from view.
And all that he left when living was through,
Was a mountain of things he intended to do![17]
                                —Author Unknown

Get more directly involved in God's Word and kingdom work. Volunteer! Every senior Christian should
ask him or herself Isaac Watts' question—

> Must I be carried to the skies
> On flowery beds of ease,
> While others fought to win the prize,
> And sailed through bloody seas?
> —Isaac Watts [1674-1748]

God is not done with you yet—not by a long shot!

WINNING WAYS

• When the roof leaks, don't expect rooms below to stay dry. Certain circumstances, such as a leaky roof, require immediate attention lest damage become extensive. We pay a heavy price when we fail to act.

• Procrastination is more than the thief of time. It is a robber of our peace of mind and pillager of our bank account. Address the hard decisions of each day and seek solutions. This may require calling in experts or specialists. But having fewer concerns to weigh us down, our travel through the rest of the year and life itself is made easier and less stressful. Friends and family can be good coaches in dealing with difficult problems.

• The depressed person is unable to make decisions. So address that condition. Even adults may suffer from ADD (Attention Deficit Disorder), which is character-ized by inability to focus and complete actions. Write down your goals and record their completion.

One action that helps counteract indecisiveness is doing a little good to our bodies by exercising. Take action, exercise, so that our total body will work at its best. Positive results are the dividends for those who work the body in sensible activity. If you can no longer jog, then walk. If you no longer walk, then stretch or use a stationary bike or stair master. The exertion will also nourish your greater sense of well being.

• Avoiding decisions on health care will only accelerate physical decline. Don't expect health insurance to cover everything. Action, rather than inaction, makes for a longer, fuller, more rewarding life. We prepare for the future by not procrastinating about meeting our present needs.

THINGS TO THINK ABOUT:

[1] List nagging personal regrets. (Limit yourself to five you are willing to air.) Of the five, when did you begin to regard them as regrets? In each case, what made you hesitate to seize the situation?

[2] Lingering over missed opportunities can lock us into moods of disappointment and despair. Rather than dwell on past procrastination that left you dissatisfied, what attitudinal changes will make your last decades more satisfying?

[3] The Bible warns against withholding praise from those to whom it is due. We are exhorted to rejoice with those who rejoice and weep with those who weep (Rom. 12:15). What makes us hesitate to recognize, compliment, and praise the successes of others?

[4] Many seniors think they are no longer driven by a need to compete with others. But can this be a subtle sign of jealousy? Does lingering status consciousness, for instance, control the size of our trailers we own or rent, and the number of trips we take? Does such jealousy make our memory slack, cause us to miss deadlines, overlook others' high points—forget their birthdays, children, grandchildren, graduations, awards, new clothes, new car, new home, promotions, even retirements?

CONCLUSION

Becoming seniors does not guarantee we bypass Satan's ambushes. "Even the most graceful and spiritual old age can grow extremely ungraceful and rudely unspiritual."[1] Everyone likes to get a trophy. But if we let Satan bamboozle us seniors, we are at risk of becoming his trophy.

SATAN, JESUS, AND US

This book suggests ways for seniors to avoid succumbing to temptations that target folks of our age. We began noticing how seniors' temptations reflected a pattern similar to Satan's assault on Jesus in the wilderness. (Open-ended retirement schedules can compare to the wide-open expanse of the Judean wilderness where Satan tried to pounce on and pound Jesus.)

What Satan first thought of as his freedom to entice and put down Jesus actually exposed his tactics for us to discern in our own life and times.

Jesus saw through Satan's purpose to get Him to act in self-centered ways. The Devil's aim was to tumble Jesus from his godly mission. Each of Satan's temptations was progressively more outrageous and virulent.

[Satan spoke in the first temptation] no longer of what Jesus might do, being the Son of God, nor [in temptation two] of what God will do, if Jesus is his Son. [In temptation number three] he speaks of what he will do himself, if Jesus will adore him.[2]

We, of course, are at a far greater disadvantage than Jesus. Whereas Satan's goal was to get Jesus to abandon his character and divine mission, his goal in tempting us is to continue keeping us off-center. Unlike Jesus, we are born into a state of spiritual misalignment. From birth we are morally and dynamically misaligned with God. We wander astray from the womb. Our natural ego is tilted away from the Lord. We humans make self-interest our spiritual measuring tool, scale, and judge. Satan works through our ego aspirations in order to defeat and divorce us from our heavenly Father.

How to Turn the Tables on the Devil

A secret to our victory over Satan's wily ways is to remind ourselves of four Scriptural principles about temptation:
- temptation is inescapable
- temptation is not sin, but an encouragement to sin
- temptation rarely appears evil; it disguises itself as beneficial
- temptation keeps returning on different tracks.

But to just recognize clear principles isn't enough. To overcome temptation one must see to six more things, thereby bringing our "must do" list up to ten:

[1] *Exercise common sense*

Nip bad habits in the bud by recognizing their early symptoms.

[2] *Keep in close touch with God*

The petition, "lead us not into temptation," reminds

us that reliance on Christ is crucial to overcoming Satan's assaults on godly living.

[3] *Discern where we are weak; concentrate on our strengths*

Satan will jump the fence at our lowest points. Keep up your spiritual guard by being daily in Scripture and prayer.

[4] *Keep temptation in the perspective of God's purposes, His "Big Picture"*
We may lose a battle here and there, but the war's final victory is assured. God is ready, willing, and able to give us the strength we lack of ourselves.

[5] *Examine our defeats*

We learn from our mistakes. Begin by reexamining one defeat. For instance, consider the erosion on our inner growth by being passive television watchers. Conversation with God before an open Bible will give us strength to face struggles and sorrows in ways another network sitcom or soap opera will never do.

[6] *Recognize that Satan is no match for our Lord's power*

The Devil's tail is not red fabric, but the fabricated tale that he has unlimited power.

GEAR DOWN, BUT DON'T GIVE UP

Christians believe that God's moral standards are for all phases of life, for the last half no less than for the first half. But the Bible is more than law; it is history. Its recorded experience, as well as its precepts, provide examples for us. And it is gospel: Good news prevails at the beginning and end, and that can energize us.

Take heart from two Old Testament characters, Saul and Jacob. Saul's weakness was pride, Jacob's was depression. King Saul was a "good apple" at the beginning of his career, but in his old age he turned rotten. Jacob, however, showed a reverse pattern. In his youth, Jacob was a shyster. His was a "bad apple" start. But when a senior, through God's grace, Jacob turned out to be a landmark in godly living. The earlier supplanter became a prince with God.

Temptations test our life and growth in Christ and would make that center no longer hold. Yes, we should use the best available insights for understanding our psycho-emotional condition. But don't forget the center—and its exercises: prayer, Bible study, Christian fellowship, and service.

At any age the most effective stimulant to a repentant and sensitized conscience is Scripture. Along with the sacraments, God's Word is the Holy Spirit's effective instrument in leading us in a life that relies on God's grace, in Christ.

THE HOME STRETCH

Not only does each day bring its own temptation, but each transition in life has its particular temptations. Fourteen major ones were opened for our consideration.

How much better life becomes, how much more we can glorify God when we rely on the Lord's help and presence in our daily lives. Our last decades can continue with initiative, creativity, and spiritual purpose. We were not meant to travel in moral ruts. Make each year we live another victory lap for Christ .

> What a wonderful thing to make the tapering-off years the capstone of one's life, when all the mistakes, bad deals, wrong turns, and mean, cruel, and spiteful actions of one's life can be pushed off the edge into the sea of forgetfulness, and one can start making up for them.[3]

APPENDIX: DEPRESSION

The origins of clinical depression are complex and treatments are being constantly revised, adjusted, and improved.

In modern medicine's history, treating depression with drugs has been slow in coming. Modifying depressive behaviors and emotional pain through drugs dates from 1949, when the positive effects of Lithium were discovered. In 1952 Reserpine, to counteract the brain chemical norepinephrine, was isolated and Clorpro-mazine and the enzyme inhibitor for monoamine oxidas (abbreviated MAO) also came into use. By the early 1960s, medications became available for use in both the major psychoses and minor "neurotic" disorders of depression.

In the 1990s, research has advanced. New compounds are awaiting F.D.A. approval, regularly. Each decade has produced a new variety of medications. The general classes of medications most commonly used in treating psychiatric conditions for depression include these:

Antipsychotic (neuroleptic) agents
Mood altering agents
Antianxiety agents

The purpose of this Appendix is not to cover these classifications of drug agents for your use, but is cited as an overview of the role of prescription drugs in treating a variety of clinical depressions. Why? So that the reader has some sense of their value in achieving relief for those of us afflicted with clinical or severe depression.

1. ANTIPSYCHOTIC MEDICATIONS

There are five basic classes of antipsychotic medications and about twenty-five different compounds currently available: Examples include Thorazine, Haldol, Prolixin, and Clozaril.

We omit any reference to the psychiatric conditions, such as schizophrenia— hallucinations (hearing voices), delusions (fixed false beliefs) and/or markedly disorganized thinking and incoherent speaking. These are beyond us here and require competent psychiatric treatment. Also, we have omitted drug treatment for the presently irreversible Alzheimer's Disease, a deteriorating neurological condition characterized by loss of neurons in the central nervous system that also evidence depression.

Bipolar Disorder, also called a manic-depressive state, is more easily managed. This is an episodic disorder characterized by an elevated, expansive or irritable mood and often psychotic symptoms. Antipsychotic medications are generally used in the acute stages of this disorder in conjunction with Lithium Carbonate. For current information on manic-depressive disorder, consult Frederick K. Goodwin, M. D., *Manic Depressive Illness* (Oxford University Press, 1990).

II. Mood Altering Medications

A severe state of depression can improve through medication. Older antidepressant agents include Tofranil and Elavil. Newer antidepressants are Prozac and Zoloft. Lithium Carbonate and Tegretol also may relate to this category.

These drugs are used in cases of severe depression (an illness) with an "autonomous" quality (melancholia). Lithium Carbonate is commonly used to treat manic depressives, known for their episodic appearance and extreme mood swings. Their common side effects include tremor, increase thirst, and frequent urination. This medication has a narrow range between the ideal and toxic dose. Blood levels must be checked periodically. Older patients with heart problems may not qualify for these drugs.

III. Antianxiety Agents

Anxiety sometimes can be interpreted as depression because for among mental health professionals, "depression" has no common definition. "Depression" can describe a symptom, a mood, or an illness. The interrelationship (not interdependence) of worry and depression is close. To treat one can be to treat the other.

Depressions and anxieties that incapacitate us need medical diagnosis and supervision. Anxieties requiring medication fall into the following categories: generalized anxiety disorder, chronic anxiety disorders, panic disorders, and obsessive-compulsive disorders (OCD).

Classification of drugs for anxiety disorders often deal with specific, short-term problems, such as actors and musicians who experience performance anxiety (drugs used for panic attacks include Nardil, Imipramine, Xanax, and Klonopin). Nardil can be used in cases where a person experiences severe panic attacks with secondary avoidance behavior (e.g. Agoraphobia).

Physicians recognize that antianxiety drugs interact with certain specific receptors in the brain, suggesting that the body may produce its own internal anti-anxiety agents which these medications supplement.

Caution: Patients may not see immediate improvement with these physician-prescribed drugs. They may not take effect in hours but take a week or two to help a patient. Also, these drugs must be taken exactly as prescribed. Skipping doses to stretch the medication can be dangerous.

↜

Credit: The information cited in this Appendix is based on information supplied by R. Gregory Rohs, M.D., Director of Behavioral Services, The Christ Hospital, Cincinnati, Ohio. Thanks, also, to licensed pharmacist Lee Shafer of Tamaqua, Pennsylvania for checking the accuracy of this Appendix. Neither is responsible for errors in this Appendix.

ABOUT THE AUTHOR—

Author John Gilmore, who pastored for 35 years, was a Philosophy major at Temple University, a New Testament Greek major at Philadelphia Theological Seminary, a Colonial American Church History major at the Philadelphia Lutheran Theological Seminary, and a Theology major at Denver Seminary. In order, his earned degrees are A.B., B.D., S.T.M., and D. Min. His dissertation supervisor for the S.T.M. was the late Dr. Theodore Tappert, editor of *The Book of Concord* and Luther's *Table Talks*, and for the D.Min. project/thesis, the late Dr. Donald W. Burdick, whose crowning work was a commentary on *The Epistles of John*. For four years Dr. Gilmore was an instructor in the Philosophy/Religion Department of Wilkes University, Wilkes-Barre, PA.

Dr. Gilmore is author of a widely used and highly acclaimed textbook and reference work, *Probing Heaven* (Key Questions on the Hereafter) [Baker Books, 1989, 1994], 416 pages. Dr. Warren Wiersbe characterized it as "the best book ever written on heaven" (April 30, 1996). Copies are available through Dr. Gilmore.

In addition, Dr. Gilmore wrote a stimulating biographical/devotional study of fourteen Old and New Testament seniors, *Too Young To Be Old* [Harold Shaw, 1992] scheduled for reprint. He wrote study notes in two Bibles: Zondervan's *Sr. Devotional Bible* (NIV) and *Life's Passages Bible* (NKJV) [Thomas Nelson]. Dr. Gilmore travels near and far to churches, schools, and conferences where he engages people's thinking more deeply about the biblical portrayals of heaven and the hereafter, and of the vitality Christian seniors can bring to today's world.

Write him for brochures which list topics and provide program information. Also, references are available. For open dates contact: Dr. John Gilmore, P.O. Box 24064, Cincinnati, OH 45224. His e-mail address is— KeruxKabin@aol.com.

ACKNOWLEDGMENTS

Every effort has been made to contact copyright holders for material that did not fall into the public domain or fair use categories. If any acknowledgment was inadvertently omitted, the Publisher and Author express regret and promise to properly acknowledge in subsequent printings.

Kind acknowledgment to cite has been granted by the following:

Lyle Schaller, *The Change Agent* (Nashville, TN: Abingdon press, 1972); Ken Dychtwald, Ph.D., *The Age Wave* (Los Angeles, CA: Jeremy P. Tarchter, Inc., 1989); Christopher Lasch, *The Culture of Narcissism* (New York: W. W. Norton & Co., Inc., 1979); Alex Comfort, *Say Yes to Old Age* (New York: Crown Publishers, Inc., 1976, 1990) reprinted by permission of Reed Consumer Books, England; thanks to the Sunday School Board of the Southern Baptist Convention to cite from Frank Stagg, *The Bible Speaks on Aging* (Nashville, TN: Broadman Press, 1981); Augsburg Fortress Publishers to cite from James D.G. Dunn, *Unity and Diversity in the New Testament* (1977); from Joachim Jeremias, *Jerusalem in the Time of Jesus*, from *Luther's Works*, vol. 54 (1967), and from Walther Zimmerli, *Ezekiel*, vol. 2 (1983); to Harvard University Press for citation from Harvey Cox, *Feast of Fools* (1969) and from Jaroslav Pelikan's *The Melody of Theology* (1988); to Bantam Doubleday Dell for referencing Raymond E. Brown's *The Birth of the Messiah* (Garden City, NY: Doubleday & Co., Inc. Copyright 1977); to Greenwood Publishing Group, Inc. for referencing Nancy J. Osgood, Barbara A. Brant, and Aaron Lipman, *Suicide Among the Elderly in Long-Term Care Facilities* (New York: Greenwood Press, 1991); to Tyndale House Publishers for referencing J. I. Packer (c), 1987, *Hot Tub Religion.* Used by permission of Tyndale Publisher, Inc. All rights reserved. Thanks to Literary Agents, A. P. Watt, Ltd., London, England, on behalf of the Royal Literary Fund, to cite from W. Somerset Maugham's *The Summing Up.* Thanks to Samuel J. Trueblood, executor of the Elton Trueblood estate, for citing from his father's autobiography, *While It Is Day*, and to Simon and Schuster for permission to cite from *The Fountain of Age* (1993) by Betty Friedan.

NOTES

PREFACE

1. Sherwood Wirt, *I Don't Know What Old Is, But Old Is Older Than Me.* [Nashville, TN: Thomas Nelson, Publishers, 1992]. 8, 54, 89, 94. Used by permission.
2. Ibid., 121.
3. Kerux Kabin Ministries is an itinerant vehicle of evangelical renewal. Distinctive interactive presentations on heaven and biblical seniors are provided for churches desiring inner growth in the areas of a Christian understanding of heaven and modern senior spirituality. Dr. Gilmore's book *Probing Heaven* and his book on biblical seniors, *Too Young To Be Old,* are recommended resources. Those interested in more information should write for brochures describing these ministries (Dr. John Gilmore, P.O. Box 24064, Cincinnati, OH 45224).

CHAPER 1—MYTHS AND REALITY

1. Adele Rogers St. John. *No Good-Byes.* [New York: McGraw-Hill Book Company, 1981]. xi, xii. Used by permission.
2. Ken Dychtwald, Ph.D. and Joe Flower. *Age Wave.* (The Challenges and Opportunities of an Aging America). [Los Angeles: Jeremy P. Tarcher, Inc., 1989). This is a definitive work on the place of mature adults in today's world. 30. Used by permission.
3. Robert South, *Sermons.* [Philadelphia: J.L. Gihon, 1853]. Vol. 1:299, 300.
4. Wayne E. Oates. *Temptation.* [Louisville, KY: Westminster/John Knox Press, 1991. 11. Used by permission.
5. Jaroslav Pelikan. *The Melody of Theology.* [Cambridge, MA: Harvard University Press, 1988]. 231.
6. Samuel Peers, editor. Alfred J. Hough poem. *Spiritual Poems.* [Birmingham, AL: Old South Press, 1920]. 49.
7. Paul Tournier. *Learn to Grow Old.* [San Francisco, CA: Harper and Row, Publishers, 1972]. 191.
8. Hume Cronyn. *A Terrible Liar.* (A Memoir) [New York: William Morrow, 1991]. 330.
9. *People.* June 7, 1976. 42.
10. Robert Louis Stevenson. *The Lantern-Bearer and Other Essays.* Edited by Jeremy Treglown [New York: Farrar, Straus Giroux, 1988]. "Crabbed Age and Youth" was written in 1877. 62.
11. Martin Luther. *Table Talk.* Edited by Theodore Tappert. [Philadelphia, PA: Fortress Press, 1967]. 158.

12. Robert M. Gray and David O. Moberg. *The Church and the Older Person.* [Grand Rapids: Wm. B. Eerdmans Publishing Co., 1962]. 13. Used by permission.
13. On the matter of sexually active seniors, see 43-47. Ken Dychtwald, Ph.D. and Joe Flower. *Age Wave.* (The Challenges and Opportunities of an Aging America) [Los Angeles: Jeremy P. Tarcher, Inc., 1989]. "Gone...is the myth of a lack of sexuality in old age. New studies show that many men and women remain sexually active well past 65—sometimes with embarrassing zeal." *Time.* Oct. 10, 1977. 28.
14. Elton Trueblood. *While It Is Day.* [New York: Harper and Row, Publishers, 1974]. 140.
15. Philip Edgecombe Hughes. *No Cross, No Crown.* [Wilton, CT: Moorehouse-Barlow, 1988]. 12. Used by permission.
16. Ibid., 32, 33.

CHAPTER 2—TEMPTED TO WITHDRAW

1. George Burns. *Wisdom of the 90s.* [New York: Putnam, 1991]. 164.
2. William M. Clements. *Care And Counseling Of The Aging.* [Philadelphia: Fortress Press, 1959]. 35.
3. Paraphrased from a Nashville, Tennessee newspaper.
4. Simone de Beauvoir. *The Coming of Age.* [New York: G. P. Putnam & Son, 1972]. 472. Cecil Osborne shared the case of a man who declined all social events, including church. His excuses were that he was tired, people were boring, stupid or hypocritical. He wanted to do something else, listen to his stereo, play his TV. "There was, of course, some validity to each of his contentions, but none was the real reason." His excuses, he came to discover, originated in his childhood. "His real reason for avoiding personal contact with others in a social setting was because they made him feel inferior and insecure. He simply found reasons for avoiding the anxiety-producing situation." As a child and brother he had a sense of being alienated by his father and of being excluded by his friends. He had no close friends with whom he could relate. Cecil Osborne. *The Art of Understanding Yourself.* [Grand Rapids: Zondervan Publishing House, 1967]). 37-38. Used by permission.
5. Many friars were medieval social activists. See John T. McNeill. *A History of the Cure of Souls.* [New York: Harper and Row, 1951]. 139-140. In the fourth century, Chrysostom spent six years as a monk [T. R. McKibbons, *The Expository Times.* June, 1982. 265]. See Jurgen Moltmann. *The Church in the Power of the Holy Spirit.* [New York: Harper and Row, 1977]. 322-323.
6. *The Cincinnati Enquirer.* Feb. 20, 1992: A-2.
7. Gray and Moberg. *The Church and the Older Person.* 41, 97-109.
8. Steve Kemme. "95 Year Old Retires Again." *The Cincinnati*

Enquirer. Feb. 24, 1994: B-1.

9. Gray and Moberg. *The Church and the Older Person.*

10. de Beauvoir. *Age.* 471.

11. Karen Garloch, "Church going boosts immunity." *The Cincinnati Enquirer.* Oct. 24, 1997: D-4.

12. *Ministry.* Reformed Theological Seminary. Vol. 13, No. 1, Spring, 1994. 4.

13. *Time,* Jan. 14, 1974. 58.

14. J. E. Hodder Williams. *The Life of Sir George Williams.* [New York: A.C. Armstrong & Son, 1906]. 302- 303.

15. Ibid. 306- 307.

16. Ibid. 317.

Chapter 3—Tempted to be Bossy

1. Tournier. *Learn to Grow Old.* 198.

2. Moltmann. *The Church in the Power of the Holy Spirit.* 106.

3. Simone de Beauvoir. *Memoirs of a Dutiful Daughter.* Translated by James Kirkup. [New York: Harper Colophon Books, 1958, 1959]. 56.

4. Betty Friedan. *The Fountain of Age.* [Simon and Schuster, 1993]. 144.

5. Wayne E. Oates. *Temptation.* 32-33.

6. Tournier. *Learn to Grow Old.* 118,119,130.

7. Frank Stagg. *The Bible Speaks on Aging.* [Nashville, TN: Broadman Press. 1981]. 59- 60.

8. Malcolm Muggeridge. *Jesus Rediscovered.* [Garden City, NY: Doubleday & Co., Inc., 1969]. 41, 96.

9. Stagg. *The Bible Speaks on Aging.* 56.

10. Howard E. Butt, Jr. *The Velvet Covered Brick.* [New York: Harper and Row, Publishers, 1973]. 18-19, 93.

Chapter 4— Tempted to be Indifferent

1. Jacques Ellul. *The Meaning of the City.* [Grand Rapids: Wm. B. Eerdmans Publishing Co., 1970]. 114. Used by permission.

2. In the first temptation Jesus was coaxed into make fresh loaves of bread from rocks for personal advantage. But Jesus was not going to use His deity to get out of a jam.

    His second temptation was an attempt to get Jesus to substitute leaning on a divine promise for living by a divine precept. But He would not violate the injunction to desist putting God's veracity to the test. Getting Jesus to think about the sensation of being caught by angels would have been a reliance on their intervention for selfish purposes. On the Temple's East side was a "Beautiful Gate." Satan suggested—Why not make a "beautiful landing" on the South side? On the Temple roof Jesus was tempted to come down from a high point of consecration.

Later, on the cross He was tempted to cease His ordeal and come down from the high point of suffering.

The third temptation was Satan's attempt to focus on the immediate realization of his mission, avoiding the misery involved in suffering and dying to achieve it. The adoration of the various nations of the world was a great goal of His incarnation. Satan's offer was to enjoy the end without going through the bitter means. Satan's offer to direct the adulation of millions without subjecting himself to the misery of dying on a cross put Jesus' pre-birth commitment to the cross to the test.

3. David O. Moberg. *Inasmuch.* [Grand Rapids: Wm. B. Eerdmans Publishing Co., 1965]. 22.

4. Weigle, C. F. "No One Ever Cared for Me Like Jesus." 1932. Hall-Mack Co. *Church Service Hymns.* Compiled by Homer Rodenhearer/Word, Inc. 1948, 1976.

5. Moltmann. *The Church in the Power of the Spirit.* 166.

6. Muggeridge. *Jesus Rediscovered.* 68.

7. Lew Moores. "Putting a Cap on Apathy." *The Cincinnati Enquirer.* August 31, 1995: C-6.

8. Edward Gibbon. *The Decline and Fall of the Roman Empire.* [London: Frederick Warne and Co., 1890].Vol. 1:333.

9. Henry P. Liddon. *The Divinity of our Lord and Saviour Jesus Christ.* [London: Rivingtons, 1867, 1889]. 137.

10. Stagg. *The Bible Speaks on Aging.* 21,22,25.

11. Walther Zimmerli [1907-1983]. *Ezekiel 2* (Chapters 25-48). Translated by James D. Martin [Philadelphia, PA: Fortress Press, 1983]. Vol. 2:58, 59.

CHAPTER 5—TEMPTED TO BE GULLIBLE

1. Dan Horn. *The Cincinnati Post.* July 23, 1994: A-1.

2. Senior suspicion has been recognized from early English Protestant English Christianity: See William Bridge. *The Works of William Bridge.* [Beaver Falls, PA: Soli Deo Gloria Publications, 1845, 1989]. Vol. 5: 183 (written in 1667). Also R. L. Stevenson. *Lantern-Bearer.* 62.

3. de Beauvoir. *Coming of Age.* 393.

4. The poem was listed as unknown as far back as 1936. The present form of the poem has been altered from the original form to fit with current English usage. Found in the poetry collection of Hazel Felleman, compiler/editor, *The Best Loved Poems of the American People.* [Garden City, NY: Doubleday & Co., Inc. 1936]. 482.

5. *The Philadelphia Inquirer.* Oct. 14, 1979: A-1, A-6.

6. P. E. Hughes. *No Cross, No Crown.* 9.

7. Abraham Kuyper. *The Work of the Holy Spirit.* [Grand Rapids: Christian Classics, 1972]. 196. 17th Chapter, Sec. 34.

8. Brought out in the Goodspeed, Moffatt, GNB, RSV, NAB, NIV translations of 2 Cor. 11:3.
9. Peter Taylor Forsyth. *Positive Preaching and the Modern Mind.* [Grand Rapids: Wm. B. Eerdmans Publishing Co., 1907, 1964. 41.
10. John Calvin. *Institutes of the Christian Religion.* IV, 9:5. Beveridge translation.
11. Alan P. F. Sell. *Theology in Turmoil.* [Grand Rapids: Baker Book House, 1986]. 141.
12. Henry Bavinck. [1854-1921] *The Philosophy of Revelation.* [New York: Longmans, Green and Co., 1909]. 226.
13. Raymond E. Brown. *The Epistles of John.* (The Anchor Bible). [Garden City, NY: Doubleday and Company, Inc., 1982]. 494.

CHAPTER 6—TEMPTED TO LIVE IN THE PAST

1. Win Arn with Charles Arn. *Live Long & Love It.* [Tyndale House, 1991]. 73.
2. G. C. Berkouwer. *The Church.* [Grand Rapids: Wm. B. Eerdmans Publishing Co., 1976]. 186.
3. John Howard Raven. *The History of the Religion of Israel.* [Grand Rapids: Baker Book House, 1933, 1979]. 74.
4. Paul F. Schmidt. *Coping with Difficult People.* [Philadelphia, PA: Westminster Press, 1980]. 37.
5. Paul Tournier. *A Place for You.* [London: SCM Press, Ltd., 1968]. 58.
6. Austin Farrer. *Triple Victory.* [Crowley Publications.] 59-60. Used by permission.
7. Marvin Vincent. *Word Studies in the New Testament.* [New York: Charles Scribner's Sons, 1886], Vol. 1:28. Vincent says "pinnacle" has the sense of "wing." Schlatter preferred "balcony" and Gustav Dallman "corner."
8. Konrad Weiss. *pous.* TDNT, Vol. 6 (1968): 628.
9. Farrer. *Triple Victory.* [Crowley Publications. 1965]. 55.
10. J. Moltmann. *The Theology of Hope.* [New York: Harper and Row, Publishers, 1967]. 26. Moltmann. *Power of the Spirit.* 281.

CHAPTER 7—TEMPTED TO FANTASIZE

1. Robert South [1634-1716]. *Sermons.* Vol. 1: 299.
2. Harvey Cox. *The Feast of Fools.* [Cambridge, MA: Harvard University Press, 1969]. 62. Oates. *Temptation.* 72— "Fantasy is a product of imagination. It can be a substitute for action, or it can be preparation or planning for later action….Fantasy that is close to reality might more accurately be called keen anticipation…. Fantasy that is sealed off from reality is thereby cut off from the ethical perceptions of the person and may break forth in irrational action. Then testing of a fantasy against reality never happens." Used by permission of author.
3. Karl Barth. *Church Dogmatics*, III/1. G. W. Bromiley, translator

[Edinburgh: T & T Clark, 1957]. 91. Used by permission.

4. Tournier. *Learn to Grow Old.* 184.

5. Ruth Carter Stapleton. *The Gift of Inner Healing.* [Waco, TX: Word, 1976]. 30, 38, 97, 98.

6. Farrer. *Triple Victory.* 54, 74.

7. Wolfhart Pannenberg. *Jesus, God, and Man.* 2nd ed. [Phila., PA: Westminster Press, 1977]. 94.

8. Moltmann. *Power of the Spirit.* 190.

9. de Beauvoir. *Coming of Age.* 372.

10. Oates. *Temptation.* 72. Used by permission.

11. Victor E. Frankl. *Man's Search for Meaning.* [New York: Pocket Books, 1963]. 44-45.

12. Paul Tournier. *The Strong and the Weak.* [London: SCM Press, Ltd., 1963]. 65.

13. Chrisopher Lasch. *The Culture of Narcissism.* [New York, New York: W. W. Norton, 1979], 209. Used by permission.

14. Augustus Hopkins Strong. *Autobiography of Augustus Hopkins Strong.* Edited by Crerar Douglas. [© 1981 Judson Press and Company, Inc., Valley Forge, PA.]. 333. Used by permission.

15. Ibid. 333.

16. Jude 8—"filthy dreamers" (KJV). The dreaming is probably linked with defilement of the flesh. Thus, it is as much linked to erotic contemplations as well as to evocative revelations. The dreaming spokespersons gave way to filthy and false imaginings.

17. W. Somerset Maugham. *The Summing Up.* [New York: The New American Library, 1938, 1964]. 37.

18. de Beauvoir. *Coming of Age.* 292, 324, 325.

CHAPTER 8—TEMPTED TO COMPLAIN

1. Author unknown. "Little Seed." Borrowed from Miner Congregational Church Newsletter, Wilkes-Barre, PA. July, 1962.

2. Complaint Psalms: [1] Personal—Psalms 5, 6, 13, 22, 28, 38, 43, 54, 61. [2] Corporate—Psalms 44, 74, 80, 83, 94.

3. Tim Stafford. *As Our Years Increase.* [New York: Harper Paperback. 1989, 1991]. 143.

4. de Beauvoir. *Coming of Age.* 452, 401.

5. *The Christian Ministry.* March, 1971. 30.

6. de Beauvoir. *Coming of Age.* 302.

7. Merrill F. Unger and William White, Jr. *Expository Dictionary of the Old Testament.* [Nashville, TV: Thomas Nelson Publishers, 1980]. 245.

8. Richard C. Trench. *Poems.* [New York: Redfield, 1856]. 113. Chidiock Tichbourne's poem reflects the pessimism of some today:

    My prime of youth is but a frost of cares,
    My feast of joy is but a dish of pain,

My crop of corn is but a field of tares,
And all my good is but vain hope of gain;
My life is fled, and yet I saw no sun;
And now I live, and now my life is done.
(R. S. Thomas, editor, *Penguin Book of Religious Verse.*
[Baltimore, MD: Penguin Books, 1963]). 70.

9. Wirt. *I Don't Know What Old Is...*94,33.

10. Author unknown. From Plains United Methodist Newsletter.
    Plains, PA. November, 1964.

11. Wirt. *I Don't Know What Old Is.* 112.

12. John Newton. *The Works of John Newton.* [Edinburgh: The Banner
    of Truth Trust. 1820, 1985]. Vol. 3:525. (Olney Hymnal Book 2, #60).

13. Israel's Murmur Score Card: Pre-Exodus Murmuring: Exodus
    14:9-12 (1st murmuring)
    Post-Exodus Murmuring: Exodus 15:22-24 (2nd murmuring)
    Exodus 16:1-22 (3rd murmuring)
    Exodus 16:20 (4th murmuring)
    Exodus 16:26-28 (5th murmuring)
    Exodus 17:1-6 (6th murmuring)
    Exodus 32:1-6 (7th murmuring)
    Numbers 11:1-3 (8th murmuring)
    Numbers 12:1-16 (9th murmuring)
    Numbers 13:33; 14:2 (10th murmuring)
    Numbers 16:1-50 (11th murmuring)

14. Author unknown. From weekly newsletter of Zion Lutheran
    Church. Worland, WY. November, 1972.

15. John Kiesewetter. "98 Years of Laughter." *The Cincinnati Enquirer.*
    April 29, 1994.

16. Paul Tournier. *Escape from Loneliness.* [Philadelphia, PA: The
    Westminster Press, 1962]. 127.

CHAPTER 9—TEMPTED TO GOSSIP

1. James Qualben, Ph.D. Comment on this MS. January 10, 1998.

2. John Calvin. *The Institutes of the Christian Religion.* Ford Lewis
    Battles. [Phila., PA: Westminster Press. 1960].

3. Jack Levin and Arnold Arluke. *Gossip.* (The Inside Scoop) [New
    York: Plenum Press, 1987]. 5, 42. (based on *Oxford English Dictio-
    nary*).

4. Leon Morris. *Commentary on the Gospel of John.* [Grand Rapids:
    Wm. B. Eerdmans Publishing Co., 1971], 284.

5. Benjamin Breckinridge Warfield. *Works.* [Grand Rapids: Baker
    Book House, 1929, 1981]. Vol. 3:61. Similarly, R. Alan Cole, *Mark*
    (Tyndale *New Testament Commentary*) [Grand Rapids: Wm. B.
    Eerdmans Publishing Co., 1961]. 82.

6. Frank Mott Harrison. *John Bunyan.* [Edinburgh: The Banner of

Truth Trust, 1928, 1964], 140-143.

7. Hal Morgan and Kerry Tucker. *Rumor!* [New York: Penguin Books, 1984]. 127, 128.

8. B. F. Westcott. *Commentary on Hebrews.* [New York: The Macmillan Co., 1920]. 399.

9. James I. Packer. *Hot Tub Religion.* [Wheaton, IL: Used by permission of Tyndale House Publishers, Inc. All rights reserved. 1987]. 58.

10. John T. McNeill. *Cure of Souls.* 120.

11. Author unknown. Appeared in a Sunday bulletin of Tenth Presbyterian Church, Philadelphia, PA.

12. Vincent Taylor. *Commentary on Gospel of Mark.* [Grand Rapids: Baker Book House, 1966, 1981]. 236.

13. Henry Sloan Coffin. *The Meaning of the Cross.* [New York: Charles Scribner's Sons, 1931, 1959]. 90-92.

14. Edgar N. Jackson. *A Psychology for Preaching.* [Great Neck, NY: Channel Press, Inc., 1961]. 131.

15. Helmut Thielicke. *The Waiting Father* [New York: Harper and Row Publishers, 1975]. 132.

16. Brian Whitlow. *Hurdles to Heaven.* [New York: Harper and Row Publishers, 1963]. 57.

17. Author unknown. Appeared in newsletter of Mt. Hermon Reformed Church, Philadelphia, PA. November, 1968.

18. John Bunyan. *Grace Abounding.* [Grand Rapids: Zondervan Publishing House, 1666, 1948]. 19-20.

19. Author unknown. Borrowed from St. John Reformed, Tamaqua, PA. Young-Married Sunday School class handout. May, 1980.

CHAPTER 10—TEMPTED TO BE BULLHEADED

1. Tournier, *Learn to Grow Old.* 118, 119.

2. Bruce Larson. *My Creator, My Friend.* [Waco , TX: Word Books, 1986]. 191-192.

3. Stafford. *As Our Years Increase.* 140.

4. de Beauvoir. *Age.* 469, 470.

5. John Fox. *Book of Martyrs.* [Phila., PA: The John C. Winston Company, 1926]. 9.

6. William Lane. *Commentary on Mark.* [Grand Rapids: Wm. B. Eerdmans Publishing Co., 1974]. 403.

7. Flavius Josephus. *Antiquities,* 17:6,1; 9:3; War of the Jews 1:32, 7;2:1,3. Emil Schurer. *The History of the Jewish People in the Age of Jesus Christ.* Edited by G. Vermes and F. Millar. [Edinburgh: T & T Clark, 1977]. 1:323-327. Raymond E. Brown. *The Birth of the Messiah.* [Garden City, NY: Doubleday & Co., Inc., 1977]. 166-167.

8. Joachim Jeremias. *Jerusalem in the Time of Jesus.* [Phila., PA: Fortress Press, 1969, 1975]. 96,99, 154, 157, 194, 197.

9. Ethelbert Stauffer. *New Testament Theology.* [New York: The

MacMillan Co., 1955]. 182.

10. Calvin. *Institutes of the Christian Religion*. Battles translation. Book II. Chapter 1:4.
11. G. C. Berkouwer. *Sin*. [Grand Rapids: Wm. B. Eerdmans Publishing Co., 1971]. 349. Used by permission.
12. George Bush. *Genesis*. [Minneapolis, MN: James & Klock, Publishing Co., 1860, 1976]. Vol. 1:281.
13. James D. G. Dunn. *Unity and Diversity in the New Testament*. [Philadelphia, PA: The Westminster Press, 1977]. 270.
14. William M. Clements. *Care and Counseling of the Aging*. [Philadelphia, PA: Fortress Press, 1979]. 35.
15. Richard F. Lovelace. *Dynamics of Spiritual Life*. [Downers Grove, IL: Intervarsity Press, 1979]. 199. Used by permission.
16. Moberg. *Inasmuch*. 88.
17. Eifon Evans. *Daniel Rowland*. [Carlisle, PA: Banner of Truth Trust, 1985]. 359. Used by permission.

CHAPTER 11—TEMPTED TO SELF-PITY

1. Guy Gugliotta. "At 93 Strom Thurond Still Strong Man in SC." *The Houston Chronicle*. October 20, 1996. 6-A.
2. *Star Ledger*. (Northern NJ). July 8, 1994.
3. *Time*. Nov. 8, 1976. 86.
4. *Time*. April 19, 1976. 21.
5. *Billings Gazette*. Sept. 21, 1975: 8-C.
6. James J. Lynch, M.D. *The Broken Heart*. (The Medical Consequences of Loneliness). [New York: Basic Books, 1977].
7. *Time*. Aug. 3, 1970. 50.
8. Francois Mauriac. *The Son of Man*. [New York: Collier Books, 1955, 1961]. 101.
9. *Time*. Aug., 3, 1970. 50. See Richard Burton's video on Wagner.
10. de Beauvoir. *Coming of Age*. 478,480.
11. Alex Comfort. *Say Yes to Old Age*. [New York: Crown Publishers, Inc., 1976, 1990]. 204. Reprinted by permission of Reed Consumer Books, Northants, England.
12. *Reformed Theological Seminary Ministry*. Spring, 1994. 5, 16.
13. Trench. *Poems*. 93-94.

CHAPTER 12—TEMPTED TO WORRY

1. George Keith. *A Selection of Hymns*, 1787.
2. Frank Minirth, M.D., Paul Meier, M.D., and Don Hawkins, Th.M. *Worry-Free Living*. [Nashville, TN: Thomas Nelson Publishers, 1989]. 26. Used by permission.
3. Garth M. Rosell and Richard A. G. Dupuis, editors. *The Memoirs of Charles G. Finney*. (The Complete Restored Text) [Grand Rap-

ids: Academia Books, Zondervan Publishing House, 1989].
Anxious meeting—248 (#24), 286 (#27).
Anxious room—256 (#53).
Anxious seat—115, 164 (#44), 227, 306-308, 315, 320-321, 435-436, 602-603.

4. de Beauvoir. *Age.* 308.
5. *Billings Gazette.* Sept. 1, 1975.
6. *Newsweek.* April 19, 1976.
7. For an analysis of the poem on old age in Ecclesiastes 12, see my previous work, *Too Young To Be Old.* (Secrets from Bible Seniors on How to Live Long and Well) [Wheaton, IL: Harold Shaw Publishers, 1992], Chapter on Solomon, and Endnote for expanded analysis of Ecclesiastes 12.
8. *The Cincinnati Post.* May 5, 1992: 1-A, 3-A.
9. *The Cincinnati Enquirer.* Oct. 5, 1993: A-12.
10. John Gilmore. *Probing Heaven.* [Baker, 1989; 4th printing, 1993]. (203-216), especially Chapter 12 (Can We be Sure of Going to Heaven?) The book is 466 pages. Harold Shaw Publishers is considering reprinting *Probing Heaven* by late 1998. For an autographed copy of *Probing Heaven,* send a check for $14.00 (post paid) to Dr. Gilmore, P.O. Box 24064, Cincinnati, OH 45224.
11. (Harold Shaw, 1992). Some portions are quoted in the Zondervan *Senior Devotional Bible* (1995).
12. de Beauvoir. *Age.* 468.
13. Calvin. *Institutes of the Christian Religion.* Beveridge translation. Book III; Chap. 20:4.
14. *Sunday School Times.* Nov. 20, 1920. (First appearance of the poem).
15. *American Bible Society Record.* Sept. 1970, Vol. 115, No.7. 127.

CHAPTER 13—TEMPTED TO DESPAIR

1. Gray and Moberg. *The Church and the Older Person.* 47.
2. Clara Clairorne Park and Leon N. Shapiro, M.D. *You Are Not Alone.* (Understanding and Dealing with Mental Illness). [Boston: Little, Brown and Company, 1976]. 383-384. Publisher's permission granted.
3. Nancy J. Osgood, Barbara A. Brant and Aaron Lipman. *Suicide Among the Elderly in Long-Term Care Facilities.* [New York: Greenwood Press, 1991]. 383-384.
4. William Manchester. *The Last Lion.* (Winston Spencer Churchill, *Visions of Glory.* 1874-1932) [New York: Dell Quality Paperback, 1983, 1984]. 23-24.
5. "Buzz" Aldrin. *Return to Earth.* [New York: Random House Publishers, 1973].
6. Osgood, Brant, and Lipman. *Suicide among the Elderly.* op. cit., 101.

7. *Newsweek.* August 28, 1972.
8. Elizabeth Gaskell. *The Life of Charlotte Bronte.* [London: Oxford University Press, 1857, 1961]. 94. Charlotte undoubtedly obtained solace from her sister, Anne's, poem:

> I hoped that with the brave and strong,
> My portioned task might lie;
> To toil amid the busy throng,
> With purpose pure and high;
> But God has fixed another part,
> And He has fixed it well,
> I said so with my breaking heart,
> When first this trouble fell.
> These weary hours will not be lost,
> These days of misery,
> These nights of darkness, anguish-tossed,
> Can I but turn to Thee:
> With secret labour to sustain
> In patience very blow
>
> To gather fortitude from pain,
> And holiness from woe.
> If Thou should'st bring me back to life,
> More humble I should be,
> More wise, more strengthened for the strife,
> More apt to lean on Thee;
> Should death be standing at the gate,
> Thus should I keep my vow;
> But, Lord, whatever be my fate,
> O let me serve Thee now!

9. Lucy Freeman. *The Sorrow and the Fury.* [Clifton Heights, NJ: Prentice Hall, 1978]. 63-64.
10. "Life in a Nursing Home, from the Inside." (*My World Now.*) Anna Mae Halgrim Seaver. *Newsweek.* June 27, 1994. 11.
11. Stafford. *As Our Years Increase.* 184.
12. National Health Survey, 1977.
13. Edgar N. Jackson. *Coping with the Crises in Your Life.* [New York: Hawthorne Publishers, 1974]. 37, 133. Cecil Osborne. *Release from Fear and Anxiety.* [New York: Pillar Books, 1977]. 166.
14. Richard Ellsworth Day. *The Shadow of the Broad Brim.* (The Life Story of C. H. Spurgeon). [Grand Rapids: Baker Book House, 1934, 1976]. 172-179.
15. Charles Haddon Spurgeon. *Metropolitan Tabernacle Pulpit.* [Pasadena, TX: Pilgrim Publications, 1885, reprint]. Vol. 31 (1885). 333. Ten years earlier (1875) Spurgeon was absent from his pulpit from the first Sunday in January for 12 straight weeks.
16. J. B. Williams. *The Lives of Philip and Matthew Henry.* [Edinburgh: The Banner of Truth Trust, 1828, 1974]. 413.
17. *Billings Gazette.* May 4, 1974. 11.
18. See pp. 5-7 in *Too Young To Be Old* where I deal more extensively

with the value of humor to improve life.

19. Quoted in *Focal Point*. Denver Seminary, Colorado. Spring, 1995. 7.
20. John Bunyan. *The Works of John Bunyan*. George Offor, Editor. [Edinburgh: The Banner of Truth Trust. 1854, 1991], Vol. 3:142, 143. *(Pilgrim's Progress*. Part I [1678]).

CHAPTER 14—TEMPTED TO SUICIDE

1. Alfred Lord Tennyson [1809-1892]. *Ulysses*.
2. Wirt. *I Don't Know What Old Is...* 9.
3. *Newsweek*. June 18,1990. 47; Ibid., April 16, 1973. 57. Stafford. *As Our Years Increase*. 184; Bill Blackburn. *What You Should Know About Suicide*. [Waco, TX: Word Books, 1982]. 41. Doman Lum. *Responding to SuicidalCrisis*. (For Church and Community) [Grand Rapids: Wm. B. Eerdmans Publishing Co., 1974]. 101, 104.
4. David K. Guthrie and Charles J. Guthrie. *Autobiography of Thomas Guthrie and Memoir*. [New York: Robert Carter and Brothers, 1878]. 2.
5. Robert Wennberg. *Terminal Choices*. (Euthanasia, Suicide, and the Right to Die) [Grand Rapids: Wm. B. Eerdmans Publishing Co., 1989]. 246 pages. Reviewed in *Westminster Journal*. Vol. 53, No. 2, Feb. 1991. 376-377.
6. James T. Clemons. *What Does the Bible Say about Suicide?* [Minneapolis, MN: Fortress/Augsburg Press, 1990]. 126 pages.
7. *Newsweek*. June 18, 1990. 46.
8. W. Somerset Maugham. *The Summing Up*. [New York: The New American Library, 1938, 1964]. 178-179.
9. Simone de Beauvoir. *All Said and Done*. Translated by Patrick O'Brien [New York: Warner Books, 1972, 1975] was written after her massive *The Coming of Age*.
10. Wirt. *I Don't Know....* 89.
11. C. Everett Koop, M.D. *Koop*. (The Memoirs of America's Family Doctor) [New York: Random House, 1991]. 292.
12. Rollo May. *Love and Will*. [New York: Dell Books, 1968, 1974.]. 107-108.
13. J. Douglas Trapp, M.D. *The Prime Edition*. (The Cincinnati Senior Monthly), Vol. 7, No. 9. Sept., 1995. 13—regarding physical vs. psychological impotence: "Better yet, for the 20 million or so American men who suffer from impotence, the first oral medicine should be available by April of 1998. Three experimental pills could be on the market by then: Viagra (by Pfizer, Inc.), apomorphine (Tap Pharmaceuticals, Inc.) and Vasomax (Zonagen, Inc.). Viagra blocks an enzyme that breaks down a chemical produced during sexual stimulation. Apomorphine affects chemical in the brain associated with initiating erections. Vasomax dilates penile blood vessels. (Lauran Neergaard [Associated Press]). "Impotent men may soon find solution in pills," *The*

Cincinnati Enquirer, Oct. 28, 1997: A-l.

14. Edgar Jackson. *Coping with the Crises in Your Life.* [New York: Hawthorne Books, 1974]. 145.
15. Wirt. *I Don't Know...*5.
16. Vernon Grounds. "Suicide." *Baker's Dictionary of Christian Ethics.* [Grand Rapids: Canon Press/Baker Book House, 1973]. 652.
17. Freeman. *The Sorrow and the Fury.* 35-36.
18. *The Grit,* January 25, 1976. *Billings Gazette.* Sept. 18, 1973. 1.
19. W. Reginald Wheeler. *A Man Sent From God.* (A Biography of Robert E. Speer) [Westwood, NJ: Fleming H. Revell Company, 1956]. 281.
20. Wirt. *I Don't Know....*150-151.
21. As a contrast to Augustine, read Karl Barth. *Church Dogmatics.* III/4 [1961]. 411.

CHAPTER 15—TEMPTED TO PUT OFF

1. Shakespeare, *As You Like It.* II.3.47-52.
2. *Newsweek.* April 16, 1973. 63
3. *Christian Ministry.* March, 1971. 52.
4. de Beauvoir. *Coming of Age.* 311.
5. Jean-Marc Matalon. "World's oldest person dies at 122." *The Cincinnati Enquirer.* August 5, 1997: A-1.
6. John Bartlett, editor. *Familar Quotations.* 13th edition. [Boston: Little, Brown and Company, 1882, 1955]. 512. Andre Maurois. *Disraeli.* Translated by Hamish Miles [New York: The Modern Library, 1928]. 261, 285, 351.
7. Matthew Henry. *Commentary on the Bible.* Vol. 5:483.
8. Paul Tournier. *The Meaning of Persons.* [London: SCM, Ltd., 1957]. 201.
9. Richard Baxter. *Saints' Everlasting Rest.* [London: Religious Tract Society, 1650, n.d.]. 129.
10. Calvin. *Institutes of the Christian Religion.* Beveridge translation. Book III, 12:8.
11. John Bunyan. *The Works of John Bunyan.* George Offor edition [Edinburgh: The Banner of Truth Trust, 1854, 1991]. Vol. 3:378.
12. Stafford. *As Your Years Increase.* 173.
13. Ibid., 68-77.
14. *Readers Digest.* Sept., 1978. 217.
15. Zondervan Publishing House. *Senior Devotional Bible* (NIV)1995, to which I contributed (cf. Gilmore pages 22, 386, 515, 725, 1278, and 1634). See Zondervan's *Daybreak Devotional for Seniors* which carries twelve of my devotions. See Thomas Nelson's *Passages of Life Bible* (NKJV). 1995. (697, 807, 846, 954, 1005, 1770, 1812, 1814 for my articles and notes)
16. Cushman poem. "The Secret." First Baptist Church, Pittston, PA. tract.
17. Author unknown. Poem "Tomorrow." *Inspirational and Devo-*

tional Verse. Compiled by Bob Jones, Jr. [Grand Rapids: Zondervan, 1946]. 86, 87.

Conclusion

1. Stafford. *As Our Years Increase.* 163.
2. Farrer. *The Triple Victory.* 73.
3. Wirt. *I Don't Know What Old Is.* 46.

Note: Every effort by Author has been made to contact copyright holders for material that did not fall into the public domain or fair use categories. If any acknowledgement was inadvertently omitted, the Author and Publisher express regret and promise to properly acknowledge in subsequent printings.

ORDER FORM

Ambushed at Sunset

If unavailable at your favorite bookstore, LangMarc
Publishing will fill your order within 24 hours.
✉ Postal orders: LangMarc Publishing • P.O. 33817
San Antonio, Texas 78265-3817

U.S.A. cost: $15.95 + $2 postage
($3.00 Priority mail)
Canada: $18.95 + $4 postage
☎ or call 1-800-864-1648
Fax: 210-822-5014

Bookstores: LangMarc books are available from
Baker & Taylor, Spring Arbor, Ingram

Please send payment with order:
    Books at $15.95   _____
    Sales tax (TX only)   _____
    Shipping   _____
    Check enclosed   _____

— — — — — — — — — — — — — — — — — — — —

Send ____ copy(ies) of *Ambushed at Sunset*

_____

_____

_____

Phone: _____

Check enclosed: _____